Cooking with Pumpkin

cooking with
PUMPKIN

Averie Sunshine

The Countryman Press
Woodstock, VT
www.countrymanpress.com

Interior photographs by the author unless otherwise specified
Book design and composition by Nancy Freeborn

Published by The Countryman Press, P.O. Box 748, Woodstock, VT 05091
Distributed by W. W. Norton & Company, Inc., 500 Fifth Avenue, New York, NY 10110
Printed in the United States of America

10 9 8 7 6 5 4 3 2 1

Cooking with Pumpkin
978-1-58157-268-1

To Skylar, my greatest gift. I love you beyond words! May all your dreams come true.

To pumpkin fans everywhere, you know who you are when a rush of excitement comes over you upon having your first pumpkin coffee drink of the season. You're not alone!

Contents

Introduction and Approach

There's nothing more all-American than a slice of pumpkin pie after the Thanksgiving meal. And there's nothing wrong with that annual slice of pumpkin pie, but there's so much more to pumpkin than pie filling, and it deserves to step into the limelight more than once a year.

I enjoy cooking and baking with pumpkin year-round. The scent of it wafting through the house is just so comforting. I crave the hearty flavor, and it's such a versatile ingredient to use in baking. However, I didn't realize others were as into pumpkin as I am until I started blogging in 2009.

Every fall the excitement is palpable as the first pumpkin recipes of the season make their appearance. I've discovered a whole cult of pumpkin worshipers out there who are just as passionate about pumpkin as I am. I wrote this book to showcase my love of the orange fruit.

Some recipes, like Baked Cinnamon-Sugar Pumpkin-Spice Mini Doughnuts and Pumpkin Whoopie Pies with Maple Buttercream, have a pronounced and robust pumpkin flavor. In other recipes, like Soft Buttery Pumpkin Pretzels, the pumpkin is more subtle, but it's there, creating a supple orange dough.

Pumpkin adds wonderful moisture to quickbreads, muffins, and cakes; it helps make pancakes fluffy. It makes cookies soft and chewy. It tenderizes yeast dough and makes brownies taste supremely rich, decadent, and extra fudgy.

When you begin to think of pumpkin as both a flavor and a softening and moistening superstar, your baking world will open up wide. And hopefully these recipes will inspire you to use pumpkin more than just for one day or a few weeks each year. There's nothing better than Bourbon Pumpkin Ice Cream with Chocolate Cookies and Chunks over the Fourth of July.

It is my overarching goal as a cook, baker, blogger, and cookbook author to make cooking as easy and streamlined as possible, and to create recipes that people want to make—and that they actually get into their kitchens and make—and for the results to taste spectacular.

I want these recipes to be made and for this cookbook to be used. I can't tell you how many recipes I encounter in cookbooks or online that, after reading the ingredients list or the directions, I quickly give up on because they just seem so daunting and like so much work. Sure, cooking is work, but I don't want it to feel like hard labor.

I've written the recipes in this book in such a way as to maximize success with the least amount of time and energy spent as possible. That includes not using every dish in the kitchen. We're all busy and don't have the time or desire to wash seven dirty bowls. Unless I'm making cookies or bread dough, I don't drag out my mixer, instead using one simple bowl and a whisk.

I do not send you on a wild goose chase to three supermarkets for specialty ingredients, nor do you need to order anything online. With very few exceptions, everything can be found at your regular store, and everything is budget-friendly. No $20 strands of saffron here.

The recipes were created to make modest batches of things—8 by 8 and 9 by 9 pans rather than halfsheet pans. One and a half dozen cookies, not four dozen. Not everyone has a huge family or wants a four-layer cake just laying around, good as it sounds. If you are cooking for a large family or a party or group, feel free to double most recipes. Recipes made in 8 by 8 and 9 by 9 formats can usually be doubled with success and baked in a 9 by 13 pan.

I want you to make these recipes, not just talk about making them. I have done everything possible to ensure the recipes are approachable for the average home cook and that your results will be fabulous. I know you'll feel proud serving everything you've made to your family and friends, and boy, won't they be impressed.

Key Ingredients and Tools

Ingredients

PUMPKIN

It's the star of the show, and all recipes in this book were tested with canned pumpkin purée. Make sure when selecting canned pumpkin that you choose pumpkin purée, not pumpkin pie filling. Pumpkin pie filling has added spices and sugar, and you won't get the results you want if you interchange the two. Everything in the book is made with store-bought pumpkin purée, not pumpkin pie filling. One standard can of pumpkin purée is 15 ounces, about 1¾ cups. Most recipes call for partial amounts from one can. See Tips and Tricks, no. 7, page xvi, for storing extra pumpkin purée.

To make your own pumpkin purée, halve a sugar pumpkin or other variety suitable for eating (the kind you carve for jack-o'-lanterns don't taste particularly good), scoop out the seeds, lightly oil the flesh with olive oil, and roast in a 400°F oven for 45 to 60 minutes, until fork-tender. Scoop out the flesh and purée in a food processor.

That said, in the interest of saving time, to ensure consistent results, and to make cooking with pumpkin a possibility year round and not just during pumpkin season, I don't typically cook with homemade pumpkin purée. If you like to clean and roast your own pumpkins and purée the flesh, you're welcome to try your homemade purée with these recipes. However, it's difficult to say if the measurements will need adjusting for homemade, or if the recipe will be successful overall, since the recipes were tested with store-bought canned pumpkin purée.

If you don't have access to pumpkin purée, sweet potatoes or butternut squash can sometimes be used and substituted with success. Some recipes will work better with these substitutions than others, but for those without pumpkin purée (outside the USA, it's harder to find) or for those who are feeling adventurous in the kitchen and like to experiment, I'm tossing it out as an option. After all, and you may be surprised to know, many brands of store-bought pumpkin purée are actually a blend of puréed winter squashes, not just pumpkin.

SPICES, SEASONINGS, SALT

Without the proper spices or seasoning, pumpkin purée can be pretty boring and bland. I'd rather be a little heavier-handed with cinnamon, pumpkin pie spice, and the like, than skimp on these ingredients. The recipes are nicely spiced, and I like the

balance and blends used, but of course, adjust spices and seasonings to your preferences and taste.

Some recipes call for pumpkin pie spice (available in the spice aisle, or, to make your own, see DIY Pumpkin Pie Spice, page 119) in addition to other spices, like cinnamon or ground cloves, that are already in pumpkin pie spice. I do this because some recipes benefit from a bit of extra cinnamon or an extra pop of cloves, ginger, or whatever it may be, and simply adding more pumpkin pie spice wouldn't give the desired balance and ratios.

Adding salt to desserts can be a touchy proposition, as I've learned from blogging. What one person enjoys, another may find too salty or not salty enough. Allow your own preferences and tastes to be your guide whether you add some salt, or none at all, to the sweeter recipes. In most cases salting is optional, and to taste.

SWEETENERS

Granulated, light brown, and confectioners' sugars are used most frequently. When measuring brown sugar, make sure to pack it well into the dry measuring cup. In some instances, sifting confectioners' sugar is ideal—like when making frosting—but I confess that I don't always sift.

Maple syrup, honey, and agave make excellent choices for sweetening options when you need a liquid sweetener rather than a dry one (such as adding a bit to cream cheese frosting or as a marinade for Maple-Pumpkin Broiled Tofu).

FATS

I prefer using unsalted butter so I can control the salt level in the recipe. I use coconut oil or canola oil in quickbreads, muffins, and cake more often than butter because I believe it makes them softer, springier, and moister overall.

DAIRY AND EGGS

Recipes will taste better if you use at least 2 percent milk (or whole, or even half-and-half). In recipes where cream is used, either whipping cream (about 30 percent fat) or heavy cream (37 to 40 percent fat) may be used. Where noted, nondairy alternatives such as almond or soymilk can be substituted.

Buttermilk is slightly soured milk and it does wonders for adding moisture, softness, tenderness, and fluffiness to anything made with it. If you don't typically keep buttermilk on hand, adding a couple tablespoons of lemon juice or white vinegar to one scant cup of regular milk and letting it stand for 10 minutes will get you by in a pinch. You can also thin sour cream or plain yogurt with a bit of regular milk, too. It's best to make the recipe with the ingredients called for, but sometimes these improvisations are okay.

Cream cheese is used frequently in frostings, spreads, and dips. Sometimes it's okay to use light or fat-free versions, and I've noted in each recipe if it is—otherwise use full-fat cream cheese so the recipe turns out. Baking with anything other than full-fat cream cheese can be a gamble unless otherwise noted.

Sour cream or yogurt also tenderize and soften baked goods and in many cases, thick Greek yogurt, plain or vanilla, if desired, to taste may be substituted for sour cream in the interest of saving fat and calories.

Eggs are assumed to be large. Fresher is always better.

FLOUR

Unbleached all-purpose from King Arthur is what I use exclusively, with the exception of yeast doughs, where bread flour may be used instead. Bread flour has a bit more gluten in it, so dough is more prone to rise, which can be beneficial when making bread.

If using gluten-free flours, your results may differ. All-purpose gluten-free blends, such as Bob's Red Mill, are probably better suited to most recipes than, say, nut-based flours like almond flour, which are heavier, denser, and not as absorbent. What you use, and with what recipe, and how much success you have, is going to be based on trial and error, as is the case with all baking—gluten-free or otherwise.

BAKING SODA AND BAKING POWDER

Not interchangeable. Make sure you reach for the correct one; and make sure they're fresh. At a cost of a buck or two, it's not worth hanging on to a year-old box of baking soda. Toss it and start fresh.

Tools

These are the main kitchen tools I use in this book and in all of my cooking and baking, most of which you likely already have:

1. Mixing bowls—Various sizes, microwave-safe

2. Measuring spoons and measuring cups—Cups both liquid and dry

3. Whisks and spatulas

4. Baking pans and baking sheets—8 by 8, 9 by 9, 9 by 13 are indispensible; loaf pans 8 by 4 or 9 by 5; 8- or 9-inch cake pans or springform pans; baking/cookie sheets and nonstick silicone baking mats (such as Silpat)

5. Blender or high-speed blender (such as Vitamix)

6. Food processor—If you don't have one, you can likely squeak by for this book by using a blender, but I do recommend one in general.

7. Electric mixer—My stand mixer is a workhorse, but if you have a handheld, that'll work.

8. Cutting board and one high-quality very sharp knife—I'd rather have one serious knife than a whole knifeblock full of dull or lower-quality knives.

9. Oven mitt, oven timer, wire cooling rack—I have a portable oven timer I carry around the house so I am sure to hear it ring.

10. Personal dishwasher and sous chef—I can dream!

Tips and Tricks

In no particular order, eleven tips and tricks to make your life in the kitchen easier:

1. Read the recipe in its entirety, at least once, preferably twice, before you start cooking. This may seem like common sense, but on a daily basis I get emails from blog readers who start off by saying, "I didn't read the recipe carefully and just added all the flour all at once and then I noticed you said to add it in stages . . ." Sometimes these little blunders do no harm, but sometimes they will cause a baking failure, so do yourself a favor and make sure to read the whole recipe, upfront.

2. Chill your dough. If it's cookie dough, you will have a much, much more successful result if it's chilled than not. Chilled dough will not be as prone to spreading, or baking flat and thin, as warm dough. Most cookie dough can be stored for up to five days in the fridge before being used, or frozen for up to three months. If it's pie dough or puff pastry, it's imperative that it be chilled. Yeast dough is the exception to the rule, where you want the conditions to be warm so the dough can rise, but after the first rise, many yeast doughs can be refrigerated for a few days before baking. Allow the dough to come back up to room temperature, rise for an hour or so, and bake as directed.

3. To use your oven as a warm, draft-free rising place for dough, preheat oven for 1 minute at 400°F, then turn the oven off. Quickly slide mixing bowl or pan with dough in and close the door. Yeast likes temps in the 90°F range—think warm summer day. One minute at 400°F brings the oven temperature into that range; just make sure to turn the oven off after you preheat.

4. When chopping chocolate, put a piece of parchment paper on your cutting board to contain the chocolate fragments. You can use it to easily transfer the chopped

chocolate into the mixing bowl, and cleanup is a breeze. No more ground-in chocolate to scrub off your cutting board. Tuck the piece of parchment into the packaging or box with the leftover chocolate, and recycle it for the next chopping session.

5. Line your baking pans with aluminum foil, leaving an overhang. I love foil because it saves on cleanup, and by using the overhang, I can transfer the whole slab of bars or entire cake onto a cutting board for easy slicing.

6. I don't slice things in a pan, ever. It scratches the pan, and as a food blogger and photographer, there's no way to get pretty servings of things when you slice and then remove the slice from the pan. People write to me wondering how I get my pieces of things to look so neat—by cutting on a cutting board, not in a pan.

7. If you don't use all the pumpkin purée from one can, transfer the remainder into a small airtight container and store it in the refrigerator for up to five days.

8. Keep a well-stocked pantry. I live in a small urban condo and happily store my mixer in my coat closet in order to make sure I have storage space for my dry goods, from sugar to flour to the occasional box of pudding, so that when the spirit moves me to start baking, I don't have to worry that, Oh darn, I'm out of brown sugar. What a buzzkill. Replenish your supplies in advance.

9. Most anything can be frozen with great success. From cookies, cakes, brownies and bars, to pancakes, bread, and mac 'n' cheese, the freezer is your friend. I'm not saying that every single item will survive the freezing and thawing process and be as perfect as it was when fresh, but it's 90 percent as good, and for a busy mom like me, that's good enough. I like knowing I have a stash of things in my freezer to draw from, as needed.

10. Don't set out to bake when you're pressed for time or know you'll be extremely rushed. My kitchen failures usually happen when I'm rushing and scrambling, so do yourself a favor and make cooking fun rather than stressful, and do it when you don't have an urgent appointment to be at in like 32 minutes.

11. Baking times are suggested guidelines and not absolutes. I tell my blog readers, "Watch your cake, not the clock." Thirty minutes in my oven and dry climate in San Diego in January is not going to be the same as your 30 minutes in Houston in July. I prefer underbaked, soft, gooey cookies; if you like them crispy and crunchy, of course bake them longer. Bake things until they're as done as you want them.

Breakfast Goodies: Breads, Muffins, and Pastries

Nutella-Swirled Pumpkin Muffins

There's a time and a place to have chocolate for breakfast, and these muffins are that time and place. They're soft, fluffy, and light without being airy. They're springy, moist, and full of hearty pumpkin flavor. Before baking, Nutella is swirled in to the top of each muffin, adding not only a pretty visual effect, but a wonderful chocolate-hazelnut flavor.

PREP: 10 MINUTES   **BAKE:** 25 MINUTES

MAKES 1 DOZEN

1½ cups all-purpose flour

1 teaspoon baking powder

½ teaspoon baking soda

1 teaspoon cinnamon

1 teaspoon pumpkin pie spice

1 teaspoon allspice

½ teaspoon ground nutmeg

Pinch salt, optional

2 eggs

1 cup pumpkin purée

1 cup granulated sugar

¼ cup light brown sugar, packed

½ cup canola or vegetable oil

½ teaspoon vanilla extract

About ⅓ cup Nutella, for swirling

Preheat oven to 350°F. Line a 12-count standard muffin pan with paper liners, or spray well with floured cooking spray; set aside.

In a large bowl, combine flour, baking powder, baking soda, cinnamon, pumpkin pie spice, allspice, nutmeg, and salt, if using, to taste, and whisk to combine; set aside.

In a separate large bowl, combine eggs, pumpkin, sugars, oil, and vanilla, and whisk to combine.

Pour the pumpkin mixture over the dry ingredients. Gently combine the batter, mixing just until the dry ingredients are moistened; don't overmix.

Divide the batter equally among muffin wells, filling each about three-quarters full. Don't be afraid to fill the wells quite high; this helps achieve big, dome-top, bakery-style muffins. It's possible you may yield only 11 muffins if the wells are very full.

Tip: When pouring batter into muffin wells, use a quarter-cup measure that's been coated with cooking spray; the batter will slide right out.

After all cups have been filled, add 1 scant teaspoon Nutella to each muffin top. Lightly swirl the Nutella into the batter with a toothpick (15 seconds in the microwave will help thin the Nutella, which makes this job easier).

Bake for 25 minutes, or until tops are domed, puffed, and a toothpick inserted into the center comes out clean, or with a few moist crumbs dangling, but no batter. Allow muffins to cool in the pan for about 10 minutes before removing and placing on a rack to cool completely.

Muffins will keep airtight at room temperature for up to 5 days, or in the freezer for up to 3 months.

Pumpkin Cinnamon Rolls
with Maple-Cream-Cheese Frosting

If you've never worked with yeast before, have no fear. The number one kitchen fear my blog readers write to tell me about is working with yeast. But after they try their first loaf of bread or batch of cinnamon rolls, I get emails saying it wasn't a big deal after all. I spell out the steps in detail here, to walk you through making the dough, rolling it up, and baking, so that you can enjoy one of these big, puffy, soft, tender rolls.

The rolls are packed with all the pumpkin flavor the dough will hold. While baking, the cinnamon-and-brown-sugar filling caramelizes and may seep out a bit, creating a sticky, gooey, wonderful caramel layer on the bottom of the rolls, which is why you should be sure to line your pan so cleanup is a breeze. The maple-cream-cheese frosting is good enough to eat with a spoon. Sweet, yet a bit tangy, and the perfect complement to the nicely spiced rolls.

When working with a yeast dough, there's little active prep, but a good bit of downtime. The rolls rise twice; the first rise is about 2 hours, and the second rise is about 1 hour. Watch your dough, not the clock. Environments vary and so will the dough, depending on temperature, humidity, and variance in ingredients.

PREP: 20 MINUTES   **BAKE:** 20–25 MINUTES TOTAL
TIME: ABOUT 4 HOURS, WITH 2 DOUGH RISINGS

MAKES 1 DOZEN GENEROUSLY SIZED ROLLS

Rolls

2½ cups all-purpose flour, plus up to ½ cup additional, as necessary (see note)

¼-ounce packet instant dry yeast (2¼ teaspoons)

2 tablespoons granulated sugar

2 tablespoons brown sugar

1 tablespoon cinnamon

1 teaspoon pumpkin pie spice

½ teaspoon ground nutmeg

½ teaspoon ground cloves

⅓ cup buttermilk

¾ cup pumpkin purée

2 tablespoons unsalted butter, diced into chunks

1 tablespoon canola or vegetable oil

1 egg, at room temperature

Note: Bread baking is weather- and climate-dependent. You may need slightly more flour in humid climates or in the summer, and slightly less flour in dry climates or in the winter.

It's possible to substitute bread flour for all-purpose. The rolls will be chewier, heartier, and less soft. You'll likely need slightly less than 2½ cups bread flour.

Filling

½ cup light brown sugar, packed

¼ cup granulated sugar

1 teaspoon cinnamon

1 teaspoon pumpkin pie spice

2 tablespoons unsalted butter, melted

Frosting

4 ounces cream cheese, softened (light is okay)

2 tablespoons unsalted butter, softened

¼ cup maple syrup

1 teaspoon vanilla extract

About 2 cups confectioners' sugar (sift if
   particularly lumpy)

To make the rolls, in the bowl of a stand mixer fitted
with the dough hook attachment (or use a large mixing bowl and wooden spoon), combine the 2½ cups
flour, yeast, sugars, cinnamon, pumpkin pie spice,
nutmeg, and cloves.

Heat buttermilk, pumpkin, butter, and oil in a
medium microwave-safe bowl for 1 minute on high;
whisk to combine. The mixture should be between
100°F and 130°F, depending on the brand of yeast
you're using. If you don't have a thermometer, err on
the side of too cool rather than too hot so as not to
kill the yeast.

Fold the pumpkin mixture into the dry ingredients in
the mixing bowl. Add the egg.

With your mixer on low speed, knead the dough for
5 to 7 minutes. This is a moist dough, but if it's too
soft and hasn't combined, add up to ½ cup additional flour as necessary, so that it comes together
into a shaggy mass. If preparing dough
by hand, knead on a floured surface for about
10 minutes. Resist the urge to overflour the dough.
A wetter, looser, moister, sticky dough produces
softer and lighter rolls. The more flour added to the
wet dough, the heavier and denser the rolls will be.

Coat a large mixing bowl with cooking spray. Using
a spatula, turn dough out into bowl, turning dough

once to grease the top. Cover with plastic wrap and place in a warm, draft-free place let rise until doubled in bulk, about 2 hours.

Tip: To use your oven as a warm, draft-free rising place for dough, see Tips and Tricks, no. 3, page xvi.

When dough is almost done rising, line a 9 by 13-inch pan or an 11 by 17-inch jellyroll pan with aluminum foil, spray with cooking spray; set aside.

Make the filling. In a small bowl, combine sugars, cinnamon, and pumpkin pie spice and stir; set aside. In a small microwave-safe bowl, melt the butter, about 30 seconds on high; set aside.

After dough has doubled in bulk, punch it down and turn it out onto a floured surface. Knead it lightly for about 1 minute.

With a rolling pin, roll it into a 12 by 10-inch rectangle.

Drizzle the butter evenly over the dough. Use a spatula or pastry brush to help distribute the butter if necessary. Sprinkle the cinnamon-sugar filling evenly over the dough.

Roll up the dough into a long cylinder as tightly as possible. Using a sharp knife, bench scraper, or piece of unflavored and unwaxed dental floss, cut or pinch off 1 dozen evenly sized rounds. Place them in the prepared pan. Cover pan with piece of foil and place in a warm, draft-free place to rise until almost doubled in size, about 1 hour.

In the last 15 minutes of rising, preheat oven to 350°F. (If you've been using the oven as a rising place, remove pan before preheating.)

Bake rolls for 20 to 25 minutes, or until golden brown, domed, set, and springy to the touch. Allow rolls to cool in pan before serving. If frosting the rolls, it may be done while they're still quite warm and fresh from the oven.

While the rolls bake, make the frosting. In the bowl of a stand mixer fitted with the paddle attachment (or use a large mixing bowl and hand mixer), combine cream cheese, butter, maple syrup, and vanilla, and beat on medium-low speed for 1 minute. Add 1 cup of the confectioners' sugar and beat to incorporate. Slowly add additional sugar until desired frosting consistency is reached. Spread frosting liberally over warm rolls. Extra frosting will keep airtight in the refrigerator for at least 2 weeks.

Rolls are best eaten fresh, but will keep airtight for up to 4 days. Warm in the microwave for 15 seconds for that just-baked taste. Alternatively, unfrosted rolls may be frozen for up to 3 months, thawed at room temperature, and warmed gently and briefly in a low oven before serving.

Tip: For an overnight or make-ahead option, after placing the sliced dough into the pan and covering it, place pan in refrigerator for up to 18 hours. Before baking, allow dough to rise in a warm, draft-free place for about 90 minutes, or until nearly doubled, and bake as directed.

New York–Style Pumpkin Crumbcake

In my opinion, there's nothing better than a thick layer of sweet, crumbly cake topping. Biting into a piece of this pumpkin-scented cake, complete with the brown-sugar streusel that adorns it, is heavenly. The cake is soft and springy, in lovely contrast to the crumbly morsels of goodness on top. They dissolve into a sugary dust in your mouth and are just so good. I could make a meal out of those delectable crumbs.

PREP: 15 MINUTES   **BAKE:** ABOUT 50 MINUTES

MAKES ONE 8-INCH PAN, 9 TO 12 SERVINGS

Crumb Topping

½ cup (1 stick) unsalted butter
½ cup light brown sugar, packed
⅓ cup granulated sugar
1 teaspoon cinnamon
1 teaspoon pumpkin pie spice
1¼ cups all-purpose flour

Cake

1 egg
¾ cup granulated sugar
½ cup pumpkin purée
⅓ cup canola or vegetable oil
¼ cup sour cream or plain Greek yogurt
¼ cup light brown sugar, packed
2 teaspoons vanilla extract
1 teaspoon cinnamon
1 teaspoon pumpkin pie spice
½ teaspoon allspice
½ teaspoon ground nutmeg
¼ teaspoon ground cloves
1½ cups all-purpose flour
½ teaspoon baking soda
½ teaspoon baking powder
Pinch salt, optional

Preheat oven to 350°F. Line an 8-inch square pan with foil, leaving overhang. Lightly coat with cooking spray; set aside.

Make the crumb topping. In a medium microwave-safe bowl, melt the butter, about 90 seconds on high. Add the sugars, cinnamon, and pumpkin pie spice, and stir just to combine. Mixture will be very granular. Add the flour and stir until combined; both large crumbs and sandy bits will be present. Set aside.

To make the cake batter, in a large bowl, combine egg, sugar, pumpkin, oil, sour cream, brown sugar, vanilla, cinnamon, pumpkin pie spice, allspice, nutmeg, and cloves, and whisk until smooth.

Add the flour, baking soda, baking powder, and salt, if using, to taste, and stir until just combined. Don't overmix. Batter will be quite thick.

Turn batter out into prepared pan, smoothing the top lightly with a spatula. Give the pan a couple of gentle raps on the counter to release air bubbles.

Crumble the topping mixture over the batter by taking up handfuls of topping and gently squeezing the mixture as you sprinkle. There will be some smaller and some larger, marble-size nuggets, as well as sandy, looser bits and pieces. It will seem like there's a lot of topping, there is.

Bake for 45 to 53 minutes, or until a cake tester or toothpick inserted in the center comes out clean or with a few moist crumbs dangling, but no batter. Allow cake to cool in pan for about 30 minutes. Lift out using foil overhang. Transfer cake to a wire rack to finish cooling before slicing and serving. Cake will keep airtight at room temperature for 4 days.

Vegan Chocolate Chip Pumpkin Muffins

These are some of the best pumpkin muffins, vegan or not—I'll put them up against muffins made with eggs and butter any day. The pumpkin gives the sweetly spiced muffins a supremely moist and soft consistency. I use coconut oil (you won't taste the coconut), but you can substitute with vegetable oil if desired. I prefer mini chocolate chips, which tend to retain a more even distribution on baking, but regular-size, or chocolate chunks, may also be used. The muffins freeze beautifully for grab-and-go breakfasts and snacks.

PREP: 10 MINUTES   **BAKE:** 18 MINUTES

MAKES 1 DOZEN MEDIUM/LARGE MUFFINS

1 cup plus 2 tablespoons all-purpose flour

2 teaspoons baking powder

1 teaspoon cinnamon

1 teaspoon pumpkin pie spice

½ teaspoon allspice

½ teaspoon nutmeg

½ teaspoon ground cloves

Pinch salt, optional

¾ cup granulated sugar

¼ cup light brown sugar, packed

¾ cup pumpkin purée

⅓ cup coconut oil, melted (vegetable or canola oil may be substituted)

¼ cup unsweetened plain or vanilla almond milk (other milks may be substituted, including coconut, soy, cow)

2 tablespoons mild or medium molasses

1 tablespoon vanilla extract

1 cup mini semi-sweet chocolate chips (regular-sized chips may be substituted, use about 1¼ cups; or use 6 to 8 ounces chopped dark chocolate)

Preheat oven to 400°F. Spray a nonstick 12-cup standard muffin pan with floured cooking spray, or grease and flour the pan; set aside. (I don't prefer the cosmetic look of liners and they could stick to muffins.)

In a large bowl, whisk together the flour, baking powder, cinnamon, pumpkin pie spice, allspice, nutmeg, cloves, and salt, if using, to taste; set aside.

In a separate large bowl, whisk together the sugars, pumpkin, oil, milk, molasses, and vanilla until combined.

Pour the wet pumpkin mixture over the dry ingredients, and stir until just combined; don't overmix. Batter will be quite thick; if yours seems too thick, add an additional small splash of milk to thin it.

Fold in the chocolate chips.

Divide batter equally among wells of the prepared pan. Each well will be just under three-quarters full (don't exceed three-quarters full or they could overflow).

Tip: When pouring batter into muffin wells, use a quarter cup measure that's been coated with cooking spray; the batter will slide right out.

Bake for 18 minutes, or until tops are domed, puffed, and a toothpick inserted in the center comes out clean, or with a few moist crumbs dangling, but no batter. Allow muffins to cool in pans for about 10 to 15 minutes before removing and placing on a rack to cool completely. Muffins will keep airtight at room temperature for up to 5 days, or in the freezer for up to 6 months.

Pumpkin Monkey Bread with Caramel Glaze

Monkey bread is the epitome of soft, gooey, sweet, sticky goodness. And the messier and more gooey, the better. This sweet dough is spiced with pumpkin, rolled into balls, dipped in melted butter, and dredged through cinnamon and brown sugar before baking. While baking, the brown sugar caramelizes, creating a luscious, dark, rich sauce that coats each piece and seeps into the cracks and crevices. And if that's not enough, additional caramel glaze is drizzled over the top before serving. It's the best possible combination of doughnut holes meets cinnamon rolls meets sticky buns. The pumpkin flavor is present, but on the milder side; the rich, buttery caramel notes dominate.

PREP: 20 MINUTES **BAKE:** 30 MINUTES
TOTAL TIME: ABOUT 4 HOURS, WITH DOUGH RISING

MAKES ONE 12-CUP BUNDT PAN

Bread

2½ cups all-purpose flour, plus ½ cup or additional, as necessary, for rolling

¼-ounce packet instant dry yeast (2¼ teaspoons)

2 tablespoons granulated sugar

2 tablespoons brown sugar

1 tablespoon cinnamon

1 teaspoon pumpkin pie spice

1 teaspoon allspice

1 teaspoon ground nutmeg

½ teaspoon ground cloves

⅓ cup buttermilk

¾ cup pumpkin purée

2 tablespoons unsalted butter, diced into chunks

2 tablespoons canola or vegetable oil

1 egg, at room temperature

Coating

½ cup (1 stick) unsalted butter, melted

1¼ cups light brown sugar, packed; plus additional as necessary

1 tablespoon cinnamon

Caramel Glaze

¼ cup (half a stick) unsalted butter

½ cup light brown sugar, packed

2 tablespoons cream or milk

2 teaspoons vanilla

Pinch salt, optional

½ cup confectioners' sugar, plus up to additional ½ cup

To make the bread, in the bowl of a stand mixer fitted with the dough hook (or use a large mixing bowl and wooden spoon), combine the 2½ cups flour, yeast, sugars, cinnamon, pumpkin pie spice, allspice, nutmeg, and cloves, and mix momentarily to combine.

In a 2-cup glass measuring cup or similar microwave-safe cup or bowl, add buttermilk, pumpkin, butter, and oil, and heat for 1 minute on high. Whisk to combine. The mixture should be between 100°F and 130°F, depending on the brand of yeast you're using. If you don't have a thermometer, err on the side of too cool rather than too hot so as not to kill the yeast.

Add the pumpkin mixture to the dry ingredients in the mixing bowl. Add the egg.

Allow machine to knead the dough for 5 to 7 minutes. This is a wet and moist dough but if it's too soft and hasn't combined, add up to ½ cup additional flour, or as necessary, so that it combines into a shaggy mass. If kneading by hand, knead on a floured surface for about 10 minutes. Resist the urge to overflour the dough, and try to live with the stickiness. Wetter, looser, moister, sticky dough produces softer and lighter monkey bread. The more flour added to the wet dough, the heavier and denser the bread will be.

Using a spatula, turn dough out into a large mixing bowl coated with cooking spray, turning the dough once to grease the top. Cover with plastic wrap and place in a warm, draft-free place to rise until doubled in bulk, about 2 hours.

Tip: To use your oven as a warm, draft-free rising place for dough, see Tips and Tricks, no. 3, page xvi.

When dough is almost done rising, prepare pan and make the coating. Spray a 12-cup bundt pan with floured cooking spray, making sure to thoroughly coat the center tube and fluted sides; set aside.

To make the coating, melt butter in a small microwave-safe bowl, about 1 minute on high; set aside.

In a separate small bowl, combine the brown sugar and cinnamon, and stir to combine; set aside.

After dough has doubled in bulk, punch it down and turn it out onto a floured surface. Knead it lightly for about 1 minute; if necessary, knead in just enough extra flour so you can work with it and roll it out.

With a rolling pin, roll it into an 8-inch square. With a bench scraper or pizza wheel, slice the dough into 64 pieces, 8 rows of 8. It's okay if they're not perfectly uniform.

Roll each square into a ball. No need for perfection here; roll quickly into rough ball shapes. It should take about 2 seconds per ball.

Tip: Flouring your palms will help prevent dough from sticking when you roll the balls.

One by one, dip balls in melted butter (quick dips, not long soaks), dredge them in the cinnamon-sugar coating, and place in the prepared pan, layering as you go so the pan fills uniformly. Replenish brown sugar as necessary. If there's excess butter or brown sugar after all the balls have been placed in the pan, pour and/or sprinkle it over the top.

Cover pan with plastic wrap and place in a warm, draft-free place to rise until almost doubled in size,

about 1 hour. (The balls will have begun to puff before you are finished dredging them.)

In the last 15 minutes of rising, preheat oven to 350°F. (If you used the oven for dough rising, be sure to remove pan before preheating.)

Bake for about 30 to 35 minutes, or until top is golden brown and brown sugar coating has caramelized and is bubbling. Allow bread to cool in pan for about 5 minutes before inverting onto a platter.

While the bread cools, make the glaze. In a medium saucepan, melt the butter. Stir in the brown sugar and cream, and after sugar has dissolved, cook over medium-low heat for 1 minute without stirring.

Transfer mixture to a medium mixing bowl and stir in vanilla, salt, if using, to taste, and half the confectioners' sugar, and whisk to incorporate or use a mixer. Slowly add additional sugar until desired consistency is reached. Liberally pour glaze over the bread (more than what's shown in the photos— it's okay if this gets messy!). If you have extra glaze, it will keep airtight in the refrigerator for at least 2 weeks. It will harden, but a few seconds in the microwave will soften it.

Monkey bread is best eaten warm and fresh, but will keep airtight for up to 3 days. Warm in the microwave for 15 seconds for that just-baked taste.

Tip: For an overnight or make-ahead option, after placing the buttered and sugared balls into the pan and covering it with plastic wrap, place pan in refrigerator for up to 18 hours. When ready to bake, allow dough to rise in a warm, draft-free place for about 1 hour, or until nearly doubled, and bake as directed.

Pumpkin Buttermilk Pancakes with Vanilla Maple Butter

There's something about pancakes that just makes me feel warm and cozy inside, and these fluffy numbers are no exception. Although they're packed with pumpkin, they're surprisingly light, thanks to the buttermilk. I serve them with vanilla maple butter, which is as heavenly as it sounds, and takes less than a minute to stir together. My family gives these pancakes two big thumbs up.

PREP: 10 MINUTES   **COOK:** ABOUT 5 MINUTES

MAKES ABOUT 20 SMALL PANCAKES OR ABOUT 1 DOZEN LARGE

Pancakes

1¼ cups all-purpose flour

2 tablespoons granulated sugar

2 tablespoons light brown sugar, packed

2 teaspoons baking powder

1 teaspoon baking soda

1 teaspoon cinnamon

1 teaspoon pumpkin pie spice

1 teaspoon ground nutmeg

¼ teaspoon ground cloves

Pinch salt, optional

1 egg

1 cup pumpkin purée

1 cup buttermilk

2 tablespoons canola oil, vegetable oil, or melted butter

2 teaspoons vanilla extract

Vanilla Maple Butter

½ cup maple syrup, warmed (about 30 seconds in microwave)

½ cup unsalted butter (1 stick), melted

1 teaspoon vanilla extract

Caramel sauce for drizzling, optional

To make the pancakes, in a large bowl combine flour, sugars, baking powder, baking soda, cinnamon, pumpkin pie spice, nutmeg, cloves, and salt, if using, to taste, and whisk to combine; set aside.

In a medium bowl, combine egg, pumpkin, buttermilk, oil, and vanilla, and whisk to combine. Pour wet mixture over dry and stir until moistened; don't overmix. Batter will be quite thick, with lumps. Add a splash more buttermilk to thin it if necessary.

Coat a nonstick skillet with cooking spray and heat over medium-low heat to warm it.

Using a medium cookie scoop or small ice-cream scoop, scoop 1½ to 2 tablespoons batter per pancake for small pancakes, or about ¼ cup for large pancakes, into the warmed skillet.

Cook on first side about 2–3 minutes; cook on second side about 2 minutes, or until done. Repeat

until all batter is gone. Pancakes are best served warm and fresh with Vanilla Maple Butter, or use your favorite syrup.

Tip: To keep pancakes warm, place in a baking dish or on a baking tray in an oven heated to 175°F, or the lowest setting, until all have been cooked and you're ready to serve.

Before serving, make the Vanilla Maple Butter. Combine maple syrup, melted butter, vanilla, and stir to combine. Pour over pancakes as desired. Optionally drizzle with caramel sauce.

Good Old-Fashioned Pumpkin Bread

Sometimes I just want a classic piece of pumpkin bread; no Nutella swirls or salted caramel glazes need apply. This loaf is the one to make when you want a moist slice that focuses on pure pumpkin flavor. It's also the recipe to make when you're in a jam and literally have five minutes to get something into a pan and into the oven. The first eleven ingredients are whisked together in one bowl, all at once, making it extremely fast and easy to whip up. But the results don't taste fast and easy, which is the best kind of recipe.

PREP: 5 MINUTES **BAKE:** ABOUT 55 MINUTES

MAKES ONE 9 BY 5-INCH LOAF

2 eggs

 1 cup pumpkin purée

½ cup canola or vegetable oil

1¼ cups granulated sugar

¼ cup light brown sugar, packed

1 tablespoon vanilla extract

1 teaspoon cinnamon

1 teaspoon ground nutmeg

1 teaspoon pumpkin pie spice

½ teaspoon ground cloves

¼ teaspoon ground ginger

1¾ cups all-purpose flour

1½ teaspoons baking soda

Pinch salt, optional

Preheat oven to 350°F. Coat a 9 by 5-inch loaf pan with floured cooking spray, or grease and flour the pan; set aside.

In a large mixing bowl, combine eggs, pumpkin, oil, sugars, vanilla, cinnamon, nutmeg, pumpkin pie spice, cloves, and ginger, and whisk to combine.

Add the flour, baking soda, and salt, if using, to taste, and stir until just combined; don't overmix.

Turn batter out into prepared pan, smoothing the top lightly with a spatula.

Bake for about 55 minutes, or until top is set, domed, springy to the touch, and a toothpick inserted in the center comes out clean, or with a few moist crumbs dangling, but no batter. If the loaf is browning before the center has cooked through, tent with foil for the last 15 minutes of baking.

Allow bread to cool in pan for 10 to 15 minutes before turning out onto a wire rack to cool completely. Bread will keep airtight at room temperature for up to 5 days, or in the freezer for up to 3 months.

Vegan Pumpkin Bread with Brown-Sugar Streusel

If you want to make a believer out of anyone who doubts that vegan baked goods can taste amazing, this is your recipe. The pumpkin helps the warmly spiced loaf stay supremely moist and soft. I use coconut oil and it doesn't make the bread taste like coconut, but substitute with another oil if desired. The buttery, brown-sugar-based streusel is a thick and moist streusel; it bakes into the batter and turns into a chewy crust, rather than sitting on top as dry nuggets. The contrast in texture between the chewy topping and soft, tender bread is amazing. (Note that the streusel is vegetarian; to keep recipe vegan, substitute a vegan spread for the butter.) You'll never miss the eggs or butter in this pumpkin bread, which could just as easily be called cake. But since it's bread, it's acceptable to eat for breakfast, right?

PREP: 15 MINUTES   **BAKE:** ABOUT 40 MINUTES
TOTAL: ABOUT 1½ HOURS, WITH COOLING

MAKES ONE 9 BY 5-INCH LOAF (SEE NOTE)

Note: To bake as muffins, use a 12-count standard muffin pan. If making muffins, baking time will vary. Bake until muffins are domed, done, and set.

Streusel

¼ cup (half a stick) unsalted butter (or vegan buttery spread)

¼ cup light brown sugar, packed

About ¼ cup all-purpose flour, plus 1 to 2 tablespoons additional if needed

Bread

¾ cup pumpkin purée

¾ cup granulated sugar

¼ cup light brown sugar, packed

⅓ cup coconut oil, melted (vegetable or canola oil may be substituted)

¼ cup unsweetened plain or vanilla almond milk (other milks may be substituted, including coconut, soy, cow), preferably at room temperature

2 tablespoons mild or medium molasses

1 tablespoon vanilla extract

1 teaspoon cinnamon

1 teaspoon pumpkin pie spice

1 teaspoon allspice

¾ teaspoon ground cloves

½ teaspoon ground nutmeg

Pinch salt, optional and to taste

1 cup plus 2 tablespoons all-purpose flour

2 teaspoons baking powder

Preheat oven to 375°F. Spray one 9 by 5-inch loaf pan with floured cooking spray, or grease and flour the pan; set aside.

To make the streusel, in a medium bowl, combine butter, brown sugar, and flour, and toss with a fork until mixture combines and crumbs and clumps form. This is a moist streusel, but if yours seems too moist and is paste-like, add another 1 to 2 table-spoons flour, as needed, to dry it out; set aside.

Make the bread. In a large mixing bowl, combine pumpkin, sugars, oil, milk, molasses, vanilla, cin-namon, pumpkin pie spice, allspice, cloves, nutmeg, and salt, if using, and whisk to combine.

Tip: Using room-temperature milk will prevent coco-nut oil from re-solidifying, but if it does, a few small white clumps are okay.

Stir in the flour and baking powder until just com-bined; don't overmix. Batter will be quite thick.

Turn batter out into prepared pan, smoothing the top lightly with a spatula.

Evenly sprinkle the streusel topping over the top, using your fingers to break up large clumps if necessary.

Bake for about 40 minutes, or until center is set and a toothpick inserted into the center comes out clean, or with a few moist crumbs dangling, but no batter.

Allow bread to cool in pan, on top of a wire rack, for at least 30 minutes before turning out onto the rack to finish cooling completely. (Turn out carefully by tilting pan to side and shimmying out the loaf. If pan

was properly greased, it should glide right out.)

Slice bread with a serrated knife in a sawing motion, going over any stubborn patches of the crust a few times, taking care to be gentle so as not to compress the loaf. Bread will keep airtight at room temperature for up to 1 week or in the freezer for up to 6 months.

Baked Cinnamon-Sugar Pumpkin-Spice Mini Doughnuts

These are my favorite doughnuts in the whole wide world. Although they're baked rather than fried, they remind me of a pumpkin-infused version of fried mini doughnuts, and they are so addictively good. I love them even more than popular doughnut-chain doughnuts. Many homemade baked doughnut recipes are dry, airy, or overly cakey, but not these. The warm doughnuts soak in melted butter, creating dense, buttery little pumpkin pillows. The batter comes together quickly, easily, and by hand. And because they're mini, they go down so easily, one after the next.

PREP: 10 MINUTES **BAKE:** 10 MINUTES

MAKES ABOUT 1 DOZEN MINI DOUGHNUTS
AND 1 DOZEN DOUGHNUT HOLES

Doughnuts

1¾ cups all-purpose flour

1½ teaspoons baking powder

1 teaspoon cinnamon

1 teaspoon pumpkin pie spice

½ teaspoon ground nutmeg

½ teaspoon allspice

¼ teaspoon ground cloves

Pinch salt, optional

1 egg

¾ cup pumpkin purée

¾ cup low-fat buttermilk

⅓ cup canola or vegetable oil

½ cup light brown sugar, packed

2 tablespoons granulated sugar

2 teaspoons vanilla extract

Cinnamon-Sugar Pumpkin-Spice Coating

½ cup (1 stick) unsalted butter, melted

½ cup granulated sugar

1 teaspoon ground cinnamon

1 teaspoon pumpkin pie spice

Preheat oven to 350°F. Spray mini doughnut pan and doughnut hole pan (or mini muffin pan) with floured nonstick cooking spray; set aside.

Make the doughnuts. In a large bowl, combine the flour, baking powder, cinnamon, pumpkin pie spice, nutmeg, allspice, cloves, and salt, if using, to taste, and whisk to combine; set aside.

In a medium bowl, combine the egg, pumpkin, buttermilk, oil, sugars, and vanilla, and whisk until smooth. Slowly pour wet ingredients into the dry, and stir until just combined. Batter will be lumpy and thick. Don't overmix to try to smooth it out.

Spray a small spoon with nonstick cooking spray (this will help the batter slide off easily), and spoon the batter into the doughnut pan wells, filling each about two-thirds to three-quarters full. The pan is small and there is no easy way to do this without spattering. After all the wells are filled, I go back around with a paper towel or my finger to wipe off any excess batter.

When filling the doughnut hole pan (or mini muffin pan), fill each well to about three-quarters full. Fuller wells create more domed and globe-like donut holes.

Bake donuts for about 10 minutes, and donut holes for about 11 to 12 minutes, or until they have domed, puffed, and are springy to the touch. Cooking times will vary based on pan sizes and fullness of the wells. Allow doughnuts and doughnut holes to cool in pans for about 5 minutes before turning out onto wire racks.

While the doughnuts cool, make the coating. Melt the butter in a small microwave-safe bowl, about 1 minute; set aside.

In a separate small bowl, combine the sugar, cinnamon, and pumpkin pie spice, and stir to combine; set aside.

After the doughnuts and doughnut holes have cooled enough to handle, quickly dip them, one by one, into the butter and dredge in the coating mixture. Serve immediately.

Doughnuts and doughnut holes are best enjoyed fresh, but will keep airtight at room temperature for up to three days. If you don't plan to consume the whole batch at once, only dip and coat what you intend to consume to extend shelf life and prevent sogginess.

Note: Doughnut pans are available at many big-box retailers, cooking supply stores, or online, for about $10. Around the holidays, you can usually find gift sets available, with pans of varying sizes included, for a good price. If you don't have a mini doughnut or doughnut hole pan, recipe can be made in a full-size doughnut pan or in a mini muffin pan. Although you can use a regular muffin pan, part of the charm is the mini size, and for some reason they just taste better as minis.

Pumpkin Molasses Banana Bread with Browned Buttercream Frosting

I have never met a loaf of banana bread I didn't love. On my blog, I have published more than fifty different recipes for banana-based goodies and breads. There is something about bananas that makes everything they're baked into so comforting, and I always have ripe ones on hand. This loaf pairs my fondness for banana bread with pumpkin, and the result is a soft, moist, dense, and flavorful loaf. The frosting is optional, but it sure adds a wonderful touch.

PREP: 10 MINUTES   **BAKE:** 60 MINUTES

MAKES ONE 9 BY 5-INCH LOAF (SEE NOTE)

Note: Alternatively, divide batter between two 8 by 4-inch pans and reduce baking time by 5 to 10 minutes, or as necessary; or bake as a 12-cup bundt cake, adjusting baking time as necessary.

Bread

¼ cup (half a stick) unsalted butter

¾ cup granulated sugar

¼ cup light brown sugar, packed

1 egg

6 ounces vanilla or plain Greek yogurt or sour cream

1 tablespoon vanilla extract

1 tablespoon unsulphered molasses

1 cup pumpkin purée

1 cup mashed bananas (about 1½ large or
   2 small bananas)

½ teaspoon cinnamon

½ teaspoon pumpkin pie spice

½ teaspoon salt, optional and to taste

¼ teaspoon ground cloves

1⅔ cups all-purpose flour

1½ teaspoons baking soda

BROWNED BUTTERCREAM FROSTING

MAKES JUST OVER 1 CUP FROSTING

¼ cup (half a stick) unsalted butter

4 tablespoons cream cheese, softened

1½ cups+ confectioners' sugar, sifted

2 teaspoons vanilla extract

1 tablespoon+ cream or milk, optional and to taste

Preheat oven to 350°F. Coat a 9 by 5-inch loaf pan with cooking spray, or grease and flour; set aside.

Make the bread. In a large microwave-safe mixing bowl, melt the butter, about 1 minute on high power.

To the melted butter, add the sugars, egg, yogurt, vanilla, and molasses, and whisk to combine.

Add the pumpkin and bananas and stir to combine.

Add the cinnamon, pumpkin pie spice, salt, and cloves and stir to combine.

Add the flour and baking soda, and stir until just combined, taking care not to overmix, or bread will be tougher as the gluten will overdevelop; this is a fairly thick batter.

Pour batter into prepared pan and bake for about 60 minutes, or until top is golden and set, and a wooden skewer, cake tester, or knife inserted in the center comes out clean. If bread is browning a bit fast on the top, you may wish to lower your oven temperature to 325°F or tent the pan with foil during the last 20 minutes or so of cooking.

Allow bread to cool in the loaf pan for at least 30 minutes before removing from the pan and transferring to a wire rack to finish cooling.

While bread cools, make the frosting.

Place butter in a small saucepan and heat over medium-low to medium heat. Swirl the pan or stir frequently for about 5 to 7 minutes, until the sputtering, crackling, and foaming has subsided, and the butter has browned and has a nutty aroma. Watch it closely so that it doesn't go from browned and nutty to burnt and inedible.

Transfer hot butter to medium-sized mixing bowl and allow it to cool for about 15 minutes to prevent it from melting the cream cheese when added.

Add the cream cheese, confectioners' sugar, and vanilla, and whisk to combine. Based on desired frosting consistency and taste preference, add the cream, one tablespoon at a time, until desired consistency is reached, adjusting sugar and cream ratios as necessary.

Drizzle or spread the frosting over the top of the bread before slicing and serving; or slice, serve, and frost each piece individually. I prefer to use the frosting like butter and spread it liberally on the interior surface of a slice.

Store extra frosting airtight in the refrigerator for up to 2 weeks or in the freezer for up to 3 months.

Store unfrosted bread airtight at room temperature for up to 5 days or in the freezer for up to 3 months.

Pumpkin Spice Peanut-Butter-and-Chocolate-Chip Granola

Granola is one of the easiest things to make and so easy to customize based on what you enjoy and what you have on hand. Store-bought can be pricey, and never tastes as good as when it's fresh and homemade. Feel free to put your own spin on this with add-ins; suggestions are noted on the next page. When making this granola, note that the dried fruit is added halfway through baking to keep it from burning, and the chocolate chips are added after the granola has cooled to prevent them from melting.

As written, this recipe is vegan, gluten-free (use certified gluten-free oats if necessary), and soy-free. Take care that any modifications you make are suitable for your dietary needs.

PREP: 10 MINUTES   **BAKE:** 40 MINUTES

MAKES ABOUT 5 CUPS GRANOLA

½ cup pumpkin purée

½ cup creamy peanut butter

½ cup agave or honey

½ cup light brown sugar, packed

¼ cup coconut oil, melted (canola or vegetable oil may be substituted)

1 tablespoon mild or medium molasses

1 tablespoon vanilla extract

1 teaspoon cinnamon

1 teaspoon pumpkin pie spice

¼ teaspoon ground cloves

¼ teaspoon ground ginger

¼ teaspoon nutmeg

Pinch salt, optional

3½ cups old-fashioned whole rolled oats (not quick-cook or instant)

1½ cups dried fruit (I like ¾ cup raisins and ¾ cup dried cranberries)

1 cup nuts and/or seeds, optional

1 cup+ semi-sweet chocolate chips

Preheat oven to 300°F. Prepare a baking sheet by lining it with a nonstick silicone baking mat or parchment paper, or spraying very well with cooking spray; set aside.

In a large mixing bowl, combine pumpkin, peanut butter, agave, brown sugar, oil, molasses, vanilla, cinnamon, pumpkin pie spice, cloves, ginger, nutmeg, and salt, if using, to taste, and whisk until mixture is smooth and combined.

Add the oats and stir to coat.

Transfer mixture to prepared baking sheet and spread it out uniformly. Keep it piled loosely; don't pack it down. It will take up the entire surface of a large baking sheet. Bake for 20 minutes.

Remove granola from the oven and stir to fluff it up.

Add the dried fruit and optional nuts or seeds and stir to incorporate.

Keep the mixture piled loosely and bake for another 20 to 25 minutes, or until edge pieces of granola have browned and crisped, even if center pieces are less well done; granola will firm up considerably as it cools.

Allow granola to cool on the baking sheet for at least 30 minutes before sprinkling with chocolate chips and stir to disperse them. If granola is not sufficiently cooled before adding the chocolate chips, they will melt.

Transfer granola to a gallon-sized ziplock food-storage bag or into an airtight container. Granola will keep airtight at room temperature for at least 2 weeks.

Suggested Add-ins

Nut butter: Try almond butter, cookie butter spread, Biscoff, Nutella.

Spices used in the coating mixture: Mix and match the various spices listed based on what you have or add others as preferred.

Dried fruit: Try diced Medjool dates, figs, dried apples, dried apricots, dried or candied ginger.

Nuts or seeds: Try honey-roasted peanuts, salted peanuts, almonds, walnuts, pecans, sunflower seeds, pumpkin seeds.

Baking chips: Try butterscotch, white or milk chocolate, or peanut butter chips; toffee bits, diced candy bars, or dark chocolate chunks.

Vegan Coconut Oil Pumpkin Muffins

If you've never baked with coconut oil, you're in for a real treat. It makes baked goods so soft and moist. If you're not a huge coconut fan, that's okay, because unlike coconut flakes or shredded coconut, which have a very distinctive flavor, coconut oil imparts very little detectable coconut taste.

Even if you're not vegan, being able to bake egg- and butter-free is a nice option for health reasons, or for those times when you simply run out of eggs—whoops! We've all done it. These muffins are so satisfying, you'd never guess they were on the healthier side. You can also prepare this recipe as mini loaves; see note.

PREP: 10 MINUTES   **BAKE:** 18–20 MINUTES

MAKES ABOUT 18 MUFFINS

Note: The batter can also be baked as 12 muffins plus a 5 by 3-inch mini loaf, or 2 mini loaves. For mini loaves, increase baking time to 22–25 minutes.

1¾ cups all-purpose flour

1 tablespoon baking powder

1 teaspoon cinnamon

1 teaspoon pumpkin pie spice

1 teaspoon allspice

1 teaspoon nutmeg

½ teaspoon ground ginger

¼ teaspoon ground cloves

Pinch salt, optional

1¼ cups granulated sugar

¼ cup light brown sugar, packed

1 cup pumpkin purée

½ cup coconut oil, melted (vegetable or canola oil may be substituted)

½ cup unsweetened plain or vanilla almond milk, at room temperature (other milks may be substituted: coconut, almond, soy, cow)

2 tablespoons mild or medium molasses

1 tablespoon vanilla extract

Preheat oven to 400°F. Spray a 12-count standard muffin pan and half of a second muffin pan (or a mini loaf pan; see note) with floured cooking spray, or grease and flour the pans; set aside.

In a large bowl, combine flour, baking powder, cinnamon, pumpkin pie spice, allspice, nutmeg, ginger, cloves, and salt, if using, to taste, and whisk to combine; set aside.

In a separate large bowl, combine sugars, pumpkin, oil, milk, molasses, and vanilla, and whisk to combine.

Pour the wet pumpkin mixture over the dry ingredients. Stir to gently combine the batter, mixing just until the dry ingredients are moistened; don't overmix. Batter will be quite thick; if yours seems too thick, add a splash of milk to thin it.

Divide batter equally among muffin wells, filling each two-thirds to three-quarters.

Tip: When pouring batter into muffin wells, use a quarter-cup measure that's been coated with cooking spray; the batter will slide right out.

Bake muffins for 18 to 20 minutes, or until tops are domed, puffed, and a toothpick inserted in the center comes out clean, or with a few moist crumbs dangling, but no batter. Allow to cool in pans for about 10 minutes before removing and placing on a rack to cool completely. Muffins will keep airtight at room temperature for up to 4 days, or in the freezer for up to 3 months.

Cookies Galore:
Cookies and Bars

Soft and Puffy Pumpkin-Spice Honey Cookies

These cookies are moist, supremely soft, with hints of chewiness at the edges, and have wonderful flavor from being sweetened with honey. There's no pumpkin purée in them—the pop of pumpkin flavor comes from the pumpkin pie spice. The honey makes it a soft, limp dough, which must be chilled before baking so your cookies bake up thick and puffy. These cookies appeared on my blog and were an instant reader favorite.

PREP: 10 MINUTES   **BAKE:** ABOUT 8 MINUTES
TOTAL: 3+ HOURS, FOR DOUGH CHILLING

MAKES ABOUT 17 MEDIUM COOKIES

½ cup (1 stick) unsalted butter, softened

¾ cup light brown sugar, packed

1 egg

¼ cup honey (I use clover honey)

2 tablespoons pumpkin pie spice (yes tablespoons, not teaspoons)

1 tablespoon vanilla extract

2 cups all-purpose flour

2 teaspoons cornstarch

1 teaspoon baking soda

Pinch salt, optional

In the bowl of a stand mixer fitted with the paddle attachment, combine butter, sugar, and egg, and beat on medium-high speed until well creamed, light, and fluffy, about 5 minutes (or use a hand mixer and beat for at least 7 minutes), stopping to scrape down sides of the bowl as necessary. Do not shortcut the creaming process; make sure dough is very light in color and fluffy.

After scraping down the sides of the bowl, add the honey, pumpkin pie spice, and vanilla, and beat on medium-high speed until combined and smooth, about 2 minutes.

Again scrape down the sides of the bowl and add the flour, cornstarch, baking soda, and salt, if using, to taste, and mix until just combined, about 1 minute.

Using a medium 2-inch cookie scoop, form heaping two-tablespoon mounds. Place mounds on a large plate, flatten mounds very slightly with your palm, cover with plastic wrap, and refrigerate for at least 3 hours, or up to 5 days, before baking. Do not bake with warm dough; cookies will spread and bake thin and flat.

Preheat oven to 350°F, line baking sheets with nonstick silicone baking mats, or spray with cooking spray. Place mounds on baking sheets, spaced at least 2 inches apart (I bake 8 cookies per sheet). Bake for 8 to 9 minutes, or until edges have set and tops are just beginning to set, even if undercooked,

pale, and glossy in the center. Do not bake longer than 9 minutes for soft cookies; they will firm up as they cool. Bake for 9–10 minutes if you like firmer cookies.

Allow cookies to cool on the baking sheet for about 5 minutes before removing and transferring to a rack to finish cooling.

Store cookies airtight at room temperature for up to 1 week, or in the freezer for up to 4 months. Alternatively, unbaked cookie dough can be stored airtight in the refrigerator for up to 5 days; consider baking only as many cookies as desired and save the remaining dough for baking later.

Pumpkin Whoopie Pies with Maple Buttercream

Whoopie! That's what I say when I bite into these. The cookies are soft and supple, and the buttercream is thick and rich. It's the perfect filling for sandwiching between layers that are more like little pumpkin cakes than cookies. If you've never made whoopie pies before, they're so easy and yummy, you'll be hooked. And there's no dough to chill, making for a very fast cookie recipe.

PREP: 10 MINUTES **BAKE:** 12 TO 14 MINUTES

MAKES 6 LARGE AND VERY GENEROUSLY STUFFED WHOOPIE PIES. RECIPE MAY BE DOUBLED IF DESIRED.

Cookies

1 cup light brown sugar, packed

½ cup canola or vegetable oil

¾ cup pumpkin purée

1 egg

1½ teaspoons vanilla extract

1 teaspoon cinnamon

1 teaspoon ground ginger

1 teaspoon pumpkin pie spice

½ teaspoon ground cloves

½ teaspoon allspice

Pinch salt, optional

1½ cups all-purpose flour

½ teaspoon baking powder

½ teaspoon baking soda

MAPLE BUTTERCREAM

MAKES ABOUT 2½ CUPS, ENOUGH TO GENEROUSLY FILL THE WHOOPIE PIES

½ cup unsalted butter, softened

2 tablespoons real maple syrup (or 1 teaspoon maple extract)

1½ teaspoons vanilla extract

½ teaspoon cinnamon

2½ cups+ confectioners' sugar, sifted

1 tablespoon+ cream or milk, optional

Preheat the oven to 325°F and line two baking sheets with nonstick silicone baking mats or parchment paper; set aside.

Make the cookies. In a large mixing bowl, combine brown sugar, oil, pumpkin, egg, vanilla, cinnamon, ginger, pumpkin pie spice, cloves, allspice, and salt, if using, to taste, and whisk until smooth.

Add the flour, baking powder, and baking soda, and stir until just combined. Batter will be soft and on the runny side, more like cake batter than cookie dough.

Using a quarter-cup measure sprayed with cooking spray, scoop mounds of batter onto prepared baking sheets, six mounds per sheet. Alternatively, use a plastic food-storage bag with the corner snipped or a pastry bag with a large round tip.

Bake for 12 to 14 minutes, or until tops have set. Cookies will be very soft and may look underdone, but firm up as they cool. Allow cookies to cool on baking sheets for at least 10 minutes before moving them to a rack to finish cooling. Allow cookies to cool completely before filling them.

While cookies cool, make the buttercream. In the bowl of a stand mixer fitted with the paddle attachment, beat butter on high speed for 1 to 2 minutes. Stop and scrape down the sides of the bowl.

Add the maple syrup, vanilla, and cinnamon, and beat on high speed until incorporated, about 1 minute; stop and scrape down the sides of the bowl.

With the mixer running on low speed, add the confectioners' sugar slowly, about ½ cup at a time, and gradually increase mixer speed to high. Beat for 3 to 4 minutes, or until sugar is incorporated and frosting is fluffy. If necessary to achieve desired frosting consistency, you may need to add a splash of cream and adjust the sugar ratio slightly.

Apply a generous dollop of frosting to 6 cookies. Sandwich them together with the remaining unfrosted cookies, creating 6 whoopie pies.

Whoopie pies are best fresh, but extras may be stored airtight in refrigerator for up to 3 days. If you plan to store these at room temperature, the frosting may be made with vegetable shortening instead of butter.

Soft Pumpkin Chocolate Chip Cookies

I never tire of good old-fashioned chocolate chip cookies. But there's always room for tweaking the classics. In this recipe, pumpkin and complementary warming spices add a new twist to traditional chocolate chip cookies. The cookies are thick, yet light, and the pumpkin makes them very soft. Pour a big glass of milk or a cup of coffee and dive in.

PREP: 15 MINUTES   **BAKE:** 10–12 MINUTES
TOTAL TIME: 3½ HOURS+, WITH DOUGH CHILLING

MAKES ABOUT 3 DOZEN MEDIUM-SIZED COOKIES

½ cup (1 stick) unsalted butter, softened

¾ cup light brown sugar, packed

½ cup granulated sugar plus ⅓ cup for coating

1 egg

2 teaspoons vanilla extract

¾ cup pumpkin purée

1 tablespoon light or medium molasses

3¼ cups all-purpose flour

1 teaspoon baking soda

¾ teaspoon cinnamon plus ¾ teaspoon for coating

½ teaspoon pumpkin pie spice

¼ teaspoon ground cloves

¼ teaspoon ground nutmeg

¼ teaspoon ground ginger

Pinch salt, optional

1½ cups semi-sweet chocolate chips

In the bowl of a stand mixer fitted with the paddle attachment (or use a large mixing bowl and hand mixer), combine the butter, brown sugar, ½ cup granulated sugar, egg, and vanilla, and beat on medium-high to cream ingredients until light and fluffy, about 5 minutes.

Stop, scape down the sides of the bowl, and add the pumpkin and molasses, and beat to incorporate.

Add the flour, baking soda, ¾ teaspoon cinnamon, pumpkin pie spice, cloves, nutmeg, ginger, and salt, if using, to taste, and beat on low speed to just incorporate, about 1 minute.

Add the chocolate chips and beat momentarily to incorporate.

Using a 2-inch medium cookie scoop (about 2 tablespoons), form dough mounds. Place dough mounds on a large plate or platter. Cover plate with plastic wrap and refrigerate for at least 3 hours, or up to 5 days, before baking. Do not bake with warm dough; cookies will spread and bake thin and flat.

Preheat oven to 350°F, line 2 baking sheets with silicone nonstick baking mats or parchment paper, or spray with cooking spray; set aside.

Combine ⅓ cup granulated sugar and ¾ teaspoon cinnamon in a small bowl. Lightly dredge each mound in the cinnamon sugar before placing on baking sheets.

Space mounds about 2 inches apart; I bake 8 per tray. Flatten mounds slightly to ensure even cooking. Bake for 10 to 12 minutes, or until edges are set and tops are barely set, even if slightly underbaked in the center and glossy. Cookies firm up as they cool.

Allow cookies to cool on trays for about 5 minutes before transferring to a wire rack to finish cooling. Store cookies airtight at room temperature for up to 1 week, or in the freezer for up to 3 months. Alternatively, unbaked cookie dough can be stored airtight in the refrigerator for up to 5 days, so consider baking only as many cookies as desired and save the remaining dough for baking at a later time.

Soft and Chewy Pumpkin Oatmeal Scotchies

One of my favorite cookies of all time is a good old-fashioned oatmeal scotchie. I adore the contrast between the soft interior and chewy edges. The sweet pop of butterscotch works beautifully with the pumpkin and warming spices, and it's a wonderful complement to the heartier oats. If you're already an oatmeal scotchie fan, adding pumpkin is a fun twist on a cookie-jar classic.

PREP: 10 MINUTES **BAKE:** 10 MINUTES
TOTAL TIME: 3½+ HOURS, WITH DOUGH CHILLING

MAKES ABOUT 28 MEDIUM COOKIES

1 egg

½ cup unsalted butter (1 stick), softened

½ cup light brown sugar, packed

¼ cup granulated sugar

1 tablespoon vanilla extract

1½ cups old-fashioned whole rolled oats
    (not quick-cook or instant)

1 cup all-purpose flour

½ cup pumpkin purée

2 teaspoons cinnamon

1 teaspoon pumpkin pie spice

1 teaspoon ground nutmeg

½ teaspoon baking soda

Pinch salt, optional

1¼ cups butterscotch chips

In the bowl of a stand mixer fitted with the paddle attachment (or use a large mixing bowl and hand mixer), combine the egg, butter, sugars, and vanilla, and beat on medium-high to cream ingredients until light and fluffy, about 5 minutes.

Stop, scrape down the sides of the bowl, and add the oats, flour, pumpkin, cinnamon, pumpkin pie spice, nutmeg, baking soda, and salt, if using, to taste, and beat on low speed to just incorporate, about 1 minute.

Add the butterscotch chips and beat momentarily to incorporate.

Using a 2-inch medium cookie scoop (about 2 table-spoons), form dough mounds. Place dough mounds on a large plate. Cover plate with plastic wrap and refrigerate for at least 3 hours, and up to 5 days, before baking. Do not bake with warm dough; cookies will spread and bake thin and flat.

Preheat oven to 350°F. Line 2 baking sheets with silicone nonstick baking mats or parchment paper, or spray with cooking spray. Place dough on baking sheets, spaced about 2 inches apart; I bake 8 per tray. Flatten mounds slightly to ensure even cooking. Bake for 8 to 10 minutes, or until edges are set and tops are barely set, even if slightly underbaked in the center and glossy. Cookies firm up as they cool.

Allow cookies to cool on trays for about 5 minutes before transferring to a wire rack to finish cooling. Store cookies airtight at room temperature for up to 1 week, or in the freezer for up to 3 months.

Alternatively, unbaked cookie dough can be stored airtight in the refrigerator for up to 5 days, so consider baking only as many cookies as desired and save the remaining dough for baking at a later time.

Soft Ginger Molasses Pumpkin Cookies

I love soft molasses cookies that are spiced with plenty of ginger, and I frequently get the urge to bake them, even in July. I don't think of ginger and molasses cookies as only fall or holiday cookies. This recipe is for soft, crinkly cookies, not the crunchy or snappy variety of gingersnaps that you could chip a tooth on.

PREP: 10 MINUTES **BAKE:** ABOUT 10 MINUTES
TOTAL TIME: 3½+ HOURS, WITH DOUGH CHILLING

MAKES ABOUT 27 MEDIUM COOKIES

1 egg

1 cup light brown sugar, packed

½ cup unsalted butter, softened

½ cup pumpkin purée

¼ cup mild or medium molasses

2 teaspoons vanilla extract

2¼ cups all-purpose flour

1 teaspoon baking soda

2 teaspoons cinnamon

1½ teaspoons ground ginger

1 teaspoon pumpkin pie spice

1 teaspoon ground cloves

Pinch salt, optional

¼ cup granulated sugar, for coating

In the bowl of a stand mixer fitted with the paddle attachment (or use a large mixing bowl and hand mixer), combine the egg, brown sugar, and butter, and beat on medium-high speed to cream ingredients until light and fluffy, about 5 minutes.

Stop, scrape down the sides of the bowl, and add the pumpkin, molasses, and vanilla, and beat on medium speed to incorporate, about 2 minutes.

Stop, scrape down the sides of the bowl, and add the flour, baking soda, cinnamon, ginger, pumpkin pie spice, cloves, and salt, if using, to taste, and beat on low speed, just to incorporate, about 1 minute.

Using a 2-inch medium cookie scoop (about 2 tablespoons), form dough mounds. Place dough mounds on a large plate. Cover plate with plastic wrap and refrigerate for at least 3 hours, and up to 5 days, before baking. Do not bake with warm dough; cookies will spread and bake thin and flat.

Preheat oven to 350°F, line 2 baking sheets with silicone nonstick baking mats or parchment paper, or spray with cooking spray.

Put ¼ cup granulated sugar in a small bowl. Lightly dredge each mound in the sugar before placing on baking sheets, spaced about 2 inches apart; I bake 8 per tray. Flatten mounds slightly to ensure even cooking. Bake for about 10 minutes, or until edges are set and tops are domed and just set, even if slightly underbaked in the center. Cookies firm up as they cool. For crunchier cookies, extend baking time by about 2 minutes.

The cookies dome and puff considerably in the oven, and as they cool, they shrink down and become crinkled. It's important to allow cookies to cool on trays for about 10 minutes. Transfer to a wire rack to finish cooling. Store cookies airtight at room temperature for up to 1 week, or in the freezer for up to 3 months. Alternatively, unbaked cookie dough can be stored airtight in the refrigerator for up to 5 days, so consider baking only as many cookies as desired and save the remaining dough for baking at a later time.

Peanut Butter Pumpkin Hot-Fudge Skillet Cookie

I'm a major fan of all things peanut butter, and peanut butter cookies in any shape or form are at the top of that list. This giant, hot-fudge-topped cookie is soft, rich, and gooey. If you haven't tried skillet cookies yet, you're going to love how fast, easy, and fuss-free they are. No dough to chill or to shape into individual cookies. Simply smoosh this no-mixer-required dough into your skillet and bake.

PREP: 5 MINUTES   **BAKE:** 20 MINUTES

MAKES ONE 10¼-INCH ROUND SKILLET COOKIE
(OR ONE 9-INCH SQUARE PAN COOKIE)

½ cup unsalted butter, melted

1 egg

1 cup light brown sugar, packed

¾ cup creamy peanut butter

½ cup pumpkin purée

2 teaspoons vanilla extract

1¾ cup all-purpose flour

½ teaspoon baking soda

½ teaspoon cinnamon

½ teaspoon salt, optional

About ⅓ cup hot fudge, drizzled before serving
     (or Nutella, chocolate peanut butter, caramel
     or butterscotch sauce)

Ice cream, optional, for serving

Preheat oven to 350°F. Spray an oven-safe skillet with cooking oil or, if skillet is well-seasoned cast iron, butter or grease it; set skillet aside. Alternatively, cookie may be baked in a 9-inch square pan that has been lined with foil and sprayed with cooking spray. Do not use a 9-inch circular pie dish; it will be too shallow.

In a large microwave-safe bowl, melt the butter, about 2 minutes on high. Allow the butter to cool momentarily so that the egg, when added, doesn't scramble.

Add the egg, brown sugar, peanut butter, pumpkin, and vanilla, and whisk vigorously to combine.

Add the flour, baking soda, cinnamon, and salt, if using, to taste, and stir until just incorporated.

Turn batter out into prepared skillet, smoothing the top lightly with a spatula.

Bake for about 20 minutes, or until edges begin to firm up and the top surface has just set. Cookie is meant to be very soft and gooey. Don't overbake; cookie will continue to cook in the skillet after it's been pulled from the oven.

Before serving, drizzle evenly with hot fudge. Serve as is or with ice cream.

Cookie is best eaten warm and fresh, but if you're unable to consume all at once, slice the remainder into smaller pieces and store airtight for up to 4 days.

Tip: This is a great cookie to make for a party. Right before you're sitting down to the meal, stir together the batter; pop it into the oven, and bake. Dessert will be ready as the meal is ending. Break out the spoons and let everyone dig in.

Salted Caramel–Swirled Pumpkin Cheesecake Bars

The brown-sugar graham-cracker crust in these bars is good enough to eat on its own. It caramelizes while baking, and complements the swirls of salted caramel on top. The bars are a texture lover's dream, with a crisp, buttery crust, a soft dense pumpkin cheesecake layer, and drippy salted caramel. The bars are impressive enough to serve at holiday parties, and are so much faster and easier to make than traditional cheesecake—and I prefer them.

PREP: 15 MINUTES   **BAKE:** 40 MINUTES

MAKES ONE 8 BY 8-INCH PAN, 9 TO 12 SQUARES

Crust

½ cup unsalted butter

1 cup graham cracker crumbs

¾ cup light brown sugar, packed

1 tablespoon cornstarch

Pinch salt, optional

Filling

1 egg

6 ounces cream cheese, at room temperature and very soft (light is okay, microwave for 10 to 15 seconds if necessary to soften)

½ cup granulated sugar

heaping ⅓ cup pumpkin purée

2½ teaspoons pumpkin pie spice

1 teaspoon vanilla extract

2 tablespoons all-purpose flour

Heaping ⅓ cup thick salted caramel sauce (see note)

Note: For caramel sauce, see recipe page 79, or use store-bought. Do not substitute ice cream or sundae sauce made with corn syrup as the first ingredient; it's too thin.

Preheat over to 350°F. Line an 8 by 8-inch pan with aluminum foil, leaving overhang, and spray with cooking spray; set aside.

Prepare the crust. In a medium microwave-safe bowl, melt the butter, about 1 minute on high power.

Add the graham cracker crumbs, brown sugar, cornstarch, and salt, if using, to taste, and mix with a fork to combine.

Turn loose crumbs out into prepared pan and, using a spatula, pack mixture firmly into pan in an even, smooth, flat layer; set pan aside.

Make the filling. In the same mixing bowl used for the crust (no need to wash it), combine egg, cream cheese, sugar, pumpkin, pumpkin pie spice, and vanilla, and whisk until smooth and combined, or beat with an electric mixer. The softer the cream cheese, the easier the mixture comes together.

Add the flour and mix, just to incorporate; don't overmix.

Pour filling over crust.

Drizzle salted caramel sauce over batter to create swirls. To create the marbled pattern shown, drizzle caramel over batter in five wide, evenly spaced parallel lines, each spanning the length of the pan. (Think of five rows of long train tracks.) Rotate pan 90 degrees. With a toothpick, starting at the top of the pan, "draw" five evenly spaced lines through the caramel. You're dragging the toothpick perpendicularly through the first set of lines to create the marbling.

Bake for 40 minutes, or until center is set, with very little jiggle; some looseness is okay, but there should be no sloshing in the center. A toothpick inserted in the center should come out mostly clean, or with a few moist crumbs dangling, but no batter. Allow bars to cool in pan for about 1 hour before lifting out with foil overhang and slicing. I prefer to serve these bars chilled. Cover the pan with foil and refrigerate for at least 2 hours, or overnight, before slicing and serving. Bars will keep airtight in the refrigerator for up to 1 week.

Chewy Pumpkin Oatmeal-Chocolate-Chip-Cookie Bars

Cookie bars are a favorite of mine because they're faster and easier to make than individual cookies. These soft and chewy bars come together with one bowl and a whisk in less than five minutes. They're what you'd get if you combined chewy oatmeal chocolate chip cookies with soft pumpkin bars. Best of all, there's a mouthful of chocolate chips in every bite. They're perfect for feeding a crowd, serving at parties, and are a hit with kids and adults alike.

PREP: 5 MINUTES   **BAKE:** 25 MINUTES
TOTAL TIME: 1 HOUR 15 MINUTES, WITH COOLING

MAKES ONE 9 BY 13-INCH PAN, 15 TO 18 GENEROUS PIECES (SEE NOTE)

Note: Recipe may be halved and baked in an 8 by 8-inch pan. If halving the recipe, use 1 egg.

½ cup unsalted butter (1 stick)

15-ounce can pumpkin purée

1 egg

¾ cup light brown sugar, packed

½ cup granulated sugar

1 tablespoon vanilla extract

1 tablespoon pumpkin pie spice

½ teaspoon cinnamon

¼ teaspoon allspice

¼ teaspoon ground cloves

¼ teaspoon salt, optional

2 cups all-purpose flour

½ teaspoon baking soda

1½ cups whole-rolled old-fashioned oats (not quick-cook or instant)

1½ cups semi-sweet chocolate chips plus ½ cup semi-sweet chocolate chips, melted, for drizzling after baking

Preheat oven to 350°F. Line a 9 by 13-inch pan with aluminum foil and spray with cooking spray; set aside.

In a large microwave-safe bowl, melt the butter, about 1 minute on high. Add pumpkin, egg, sugars, vanilla, pumpkin pie spice, cinnamon, allspice, cloves, and salt, if using, to taste, and whisk to combine.

Add the flour, baking soda, and oats, and stir to combine. Add the 1½ cups chocolate chips and stir to incorporate.

Turn batter out into prepared pan. Bake for 25 minutes, or until top has set, edges have just begun to pull away from sides of pan, and a toothpick inserted in the center comes out clean (provided it hasn't been stuck directly into a chocolate chip!). Don't overbake; keep them gooey.

Allow bars to cool in pan for at least 15 minutes before drizzling with melted chocolate. Melt the ½ cup chocolate chips in a small, microwave-safe bowl, about 1 minute on high, and stir. Heat in 10-second bursts until it can be stirred smooth.

Drizzle over the bars. After drizzling, allow bars to cool for at least 30 minutes before slicing and serving. Bars can be stored airtight at room temperature for up to 5 days, or in the freezer for up to 3 months.

Hello Dolly Seven-Layers-of-Magic Pumpkin Bars

You're probably familiar with the traditional version of these bars, so popular at bake sales and potlucks. They go by many different names, including Hello Dolly, Seven Layer, and Magic Bars. This version includes pumpkin and spices for a fun twist on a familiar favorite. No mixer, no fuss, and they're fast and easy to prepare, making them a great choice when you're pressed for time but still need to deliver a chewy-and-gooey dessert that's sure to please a crowd. See suggested add-ins below and have fun with these.

PREP: 10 MINUTES **BAKE:** ABOUT 45 MINUTES
TOTAL TIME: ABOUT 3 HOURS, WITH COOLING

MAKES ONE 8-INCH SQUARE PAN, 9 TO 12 THICK
AND GENEROUS PIECES

½ cup unsalted butter, melted

1½ cups cookie crumbs (graham crackers,
    gingersnaps, or speculoos)

¾ cup pumpkin purée

14-ounce can sweetened condensed milk, divided

1½ teaspoons cinnamon

1 teaspoon pumpkin pie spice

1 cup semi-sweet chocolate chips

¾ cup butterscotch chips

½ cup white chocolate chips

1 cup sweetened shredded coconut

Preheat oven to 350°F. Line an 8-inch square pan with aluminum foil, leaving overhang, and spray with cooking spray; set aside.

In a medium microwave-safe bowl, melt the butter, about 90 seconds on high. Stir in the cookie crumbs until combined. Transfer mixture to prepared pan and with a spatula or your fingers, press crumbs down to create an even, flat layer; set pan aside.

In the medium bowl (same one is fine, no need to wash it), combine pumpkin, half the can of sweetened condensed milk (just eyeball it), cinnamon, and pumpkin pie spice, and stir to combine. Pour mixture over cookie crust, smoothing lightly with a spatula.

Evenly sprinkle with chocolate chips, butterscotch chips, white chocolate chips, and coconut—in that order.

Evenly drizzle the remaining half can of sweetened condensed milk over the top.

Bake for 42 to 48 minutes, or until coconut has just begun to turn golden brown around the edges, with minor toasting in the middle of the pan; or bake until desired level of browning if you prefer well-toasted coconut. It's very important to start checking the pan around 35 minutes and watch closely from there, because coconut can burn in just a minute or two, and will be prone to doing so as the baking time is drawing to a close.

Allow bars to cool completely in pan (at least 2 hours) before lifting out with foil and slicing; expedite cooling process by placing pan in refrigerator if you're in a hurry. Bars will keep airtight at room temperature for up to 1 week, or in the freezer for up to 3 months.

Suggested Add-ins

Sprinkle ½ cup of any of the following after adding the white chocolate, and before adding the coconut:

- Toffee bits
- Chopped nuts (almonds, walnuts, pecans)
- Pumpkin seeds
- Chopped golden cream-filled sandwich cookies or vanilla sandwich cookies
- Diced candy-bar pieces

Salted-Caramel-and-Pretzel Pumpkin Blondies

If you enjoy contrasting flavors and textures, these easy, one-bowl blondies are for you. Salty and sweet, soft and crunchy, with pretzel pieces baked in, adding crunch to the otherwise smooth, dense, pumpkin-spiced treats. Salted caramel sauce is drizzled over the top, both before and after baking, creating blondies that are dripping with buttery, sticky, caramely goodness. I have a recipe similar to this on my website, minus the pumpkin and related spices, and it's exceedingly popular with readers.

PREP: 10 MINUTES   **BAKE:** 30 MINUTES
TOTAL TIME: ABOUT 3 HOURS, WITH COOLING

MAKES ONE 8-INCH SQUARE PAN,
9 TO 12 GENEROUS PIECES

½ cup unsalted butter, melted (1 stick)

1 egg

1 cup light brown sugar, packed

½ cup pumpkin purée

1 tablespoon vanilla extract

1 teaspoon cinnamon

1 teaspoon pumpkin pie spice

1 cup plus 2 tablespoons all-purpose flour

2 cups plus ¼ cup mini pretzels, lightly crushed
   (see note)

⅓ cup plus ¼ cup salted caramel sauce, for drizzling
   before and after baking (see note)

Coarse salt for sprinkling, optional

Note: I crush pretzels by squeezing tightly in my fist. Some pieces will be more crushed than others; the lack of uniformity is okay.

Note: For caramel sauce, see recipe page 79, or use store-bought.

Preheat oven to 350°F. Line an 8 by 8-inch pan with aluminum foil, and spray with cooking spray; set aside.

In a medium microwave-safe bowl, melt the butter, about 1 minute on high. Allow butter to cool slightly so that the egg, when added, doesn't scramble.

Add the egg, brown sugar, pumpkin, vanilla, cinnamon, and pumpkin pie spice, and whisk to combine.

Add the flour and stir until just combined, don't overmix.

Fold in the 2 cups crushed pretzel pieces.

Pour batter into prepared pan, smoothing it with a spatula. Add remaining ¼ cup pretzel pieces in an irregular pattern to the surface of the batter for visual appeal.

Drizzle about ⅓ cup caramel sauce (just eyeball it) over the pan in a zigzag pattern. Depending on thickness of caramel sauce used, it may run together. This is okay.

Bake for about 30 minutes, or until center is just set. Watch the dough, not the caramel sauce, when judging doneness; the caramel won't fully set and

will stay glossy and bubbly. Edges of blondies will have firmed up and pulled away slightly from sides of pan. A toothpick should come out mostly clean if you can find a patch to test without hitting a pretzel or caramel. Don't overbake; they're meant to be gooey, and firm up as they cool.

Immediately after removing pan from oven, drizzle about ¼ cup caramel sauce (just eyeball it) over the top in a zigzag pattern. Sprinkle with coarse salt to taste, if desired, to play up the salty-and-sweet contrast.

Allow blondies to cool completely in pan and for caramel sauce to soak in before slicing and serving, at least 2 hours. If you can, allow the blondies to rest overnight before serving; they're best when the caramel permeates and the flavors meld. Blondies will keep airtight at room temperature for up to 1 week, or in the freezer for up to 3 months.

Peanut Butter Cup Cookie-Dough Bars

I adore all things peanut butter, especially peanut butter cups. These bars have diced peanut butter cups baked between layers of pumpkin-flavored cookie dough. The bars are flooded with creamy sweetened condensed milk before baking, creating a caramely-vanilla sauce that envelops the little peanut butter cups. The bars are fast and easy to make, and a hit with any peanut butter lover. They're dense, rich, and wonderfully soft and gooey.

PREP: 15 MINUTES **BAKE:** 25–30 MINUTES
TOTAL TIME: ABOUT 4 HOURS, WITH COOLING

MAKES ONE 8 BY 8-INCH PAN, 9 TO 12 SQUARES

½ cup unsalted butter, melted (1 stick)

1 egg

¾ cup light brown sugar, packed

¼ cup granulated sugar

⅓ cup pumpkin purée

2 teaspoons vanilla extract

1¾ cups all-purpose flour

½ teaspoon baking soda

Pinch salt, optional

About 1¼ cups diced peanut butter cups (see note)

7 ounces sweetened condensed milk (half of a standard-sized 14-ounce can)

Note: For this amount, you'll need about 9 full-size cups, diced into nine pieces each, or use the mini cups that come already unwrapped. Alternatively, use chocolate chips or peanut butter chips, or your favorite candy bar, diced.

Preheat oven to 350°F. Line an 8 by 8-inch baking pan with aluminum foil and spray with cooking spray; set aside.

In a large microwave-safe bowl, melt the butter, about 1 minute on high. Allow the butter to cool momentarily so that the egg, when added, doesn't scramble.

Add the egg, sugars, pumpkin, and vanilla, and whisk to combine.

Add the flour, baking soda, and salt, if using, to taste, and stir until just incorporated.

Reserve about ¾ cup dough; set aside.

Turn remaining dough out into prepared pan, smoothing it lightly with a spatula or your fingers to press it firmly into the pan.

Evenly sprinkle the peanut butter cups over the dough.

Using your fingers, lightly crumble the reserved cookie dough over the top in small marble-sized chunks. Some pieces will touch, and bake into each other in places; embrace the lack of uniformity.

Slowly and evenly drizzle the sweetened condensed milk over the top. Just eyeball half the can, no need to measure.

Bake for 25 to 30 minutes, or until center is mostly set, with just a slight amount of jiggle. The dough pieces on top should be light golden brown, and the sweetened condensed milk should be nearly set. Don't overbake; bars are meant to be gooey and will firm up more as they cool.

Allow bars to cool in pan for at least 3 hours before slicing and serving; do not rush this—bars need time to set, or you'll have a big mess when attempting to slice them. You can place pan in refrigerator to expedite setting time if necessary.

Extra bars will keep airtight at room temperature for up to 1 week, or in the freezer for up to 3 months.

Creamy Pumpkin-Pie Shortbread Crumble Bars

I love layered bars with lots of different textures and flavors, and these fit the bill. The shortbread crust is buttery and tender, with just the right amount of firmness and snap. It's the perfect base for the creamy pumpkin filling, which tastes like a cross between pumpkin pie and pumpkin cheesecake. The big pebbles of crumble topping add flavor, and are a wonderful crunchy contrast to the smooth filling layer. I think of these bars as the best of two worlds—a shortcut to pumpkin pie, because there's no pie crust to make, and all the pleasure of a coffeecake crumble topping.

PREP: 15 MINUTES   **BAKE:** 40 MINUTES

MAKES ONE 8-INCH SQUARE PAN, 9 TO 12 THICK AND GENEROUS PIECES

Shortbread Crust

½ cup unsalted butter (1 stick), extremely soft

1 cup all-purpose flour

⅓ cup confectioners' sugar

1 tablespoon cornstarch

2 teaspoons vanilla extract

¼ teaspoon salt

Filling

4 ounces (½ cup) cream cheese, very soft

1 egg

1 cup pumpkin purée

½ cup granulated sugar

¼ cup light brown sugar, packed

1 teaspoon vanilla extract

1 teaspoon cinnamon

1 teaspoon pumpkin pie spice

1 teaspoon allspice

½ teaspoon ground nutmeg

Crumble Topping

½ cup unsalted butter, melted

1¼ cups all-purpose flour

½ cup light brown sugar, packed

1 teaspoon cinnamon

1 teaspoon pumpkin pie spice

Preheat oven to 350 F. Line an 8-inch square pan with foil, leaving overhang. Spray with cooking spray; set aside.

Make the shortbread crust. In the bowl of a stand mixer fitted with the paddle attachment (or use a large mixing bowl and hand mixer), combine butter, flour, confectioners' sugar, cornstarch, vanilla, and salt, and mix on low speed until a sandy, crumbly mixture forms. It will seem very dry; this is okay.

Transfer crumbly mixture to prepared pan and, using your fingertips or a spatula, press crumbs down to form an even, flat layer. Pierce crust with a fork haphazardly in a dozen places so steam can escape while baking.

Bake for 12 to 13 minutes, or until crust has just barely set. It should still be white, not golden or browned, and just beginning to crust over and set.

While crust bakes, make the filling. In the same mixing bowl used for crust (no need to wash it), combine cream cheese, egg, pumpkin, sugars, vanilla, cinnamon, pumpkin pie spice, allspice, and nutmeg, and beat on medium-high speed until smooth and combined, about 2 to 3 minutes, stopping to scrape down the sides of the bowl as necessary.

Spread filling over the crust, smoothing it lightly with a spatula; set pan aside.

Make the crumble topping. In a small microwave-safe bowl, melt the butter, about 1 minute on high power.

In the same mixing bowl used for the crust and filling (no need to wash it), combine the melted butter, flour, brown sugar, cinnamon, and pumpkin pie spice, and beat on low speed until sandy crumbs form, a mix of smaller pebbles and larger marbles.

Loosely sprinkle crumbs over the filling. It looks like a lot of crumbs and it is, but they sink down into the filling while baking.

Bake for 30 minutes, or until center is set, crumb topping is just barely turning golden, and a toothpick inserted in the center comes out clean, with no gooey pumpkin filling mixture clinging. Allow bars to cool in pan for at least 2 hours before slicing and serving.

Bars will keep airtight at either room temperature or in the refrigerator for up to 1 week, or in the freezer for up to 3 months.

Indulgent Decadence: Cakes, Pies, and Chocolate

Vegan Pumpkin Cake with Pumpkin-Spice Buttercream Frosting

You won't miss the eggs or butter in this one-bowl, whisk-together, no-mixer-required cake. I love it when I can keep a recipe vegan and on the healthier side (as cakes go), without making any sacrifices in taste, and this is one of my favorite pumpkin cakes, vegan or otherwise. Note that the cake is vegan and the frosting is vegetarian, but can be kept vegan by using vegan-friendly butter and milk alternatives. I used seasonally available pumpkin-spice coffee creamer in the frosting, but another flavored coffee creamer like vanilla or hazelnut would be wonderful, or simply use milk or cream. I use coconut oil and recommend it (it imparts moisture without making the cake taste like coconut). Substitute with another oil if preferred.

PREP: 10 MINUTES **BAKE:** ABOUT 27 MINUTES
TOTAL: 1 HOUR, TO ALLOW FOR COOLING TIME

MAKES ONE 9 BY 9-INCH PAN, 9 TO 12 GENEROUS PIECES

Cake

¾ cup pumpkin purée

¾ cup granulated sugar

¼ cup light brown sugar, packed

⅓ cup coconut oil, in melted state (vegetable or canola oil may be substituted)

¼ cup unsweetened plain or vanilla almond milk (other milks may be substituted, including coconut, soy, rice, cow), preferably at room temperature

2 tablespoons mild or medium molasses

1 tablespoon vanilla extract

1 teaspoon cinnamon

1 teaspoon pumpkin pie spice

1 teaspoon allspice

¾ teaspoon ground cloves

½ teaspoon ground nutmeg

Pinch salt, optional

1 cup plus 2 tablespoons all-purpose flour

2 teaspoons baking powder

Frosting

¼ cup unsalted butter, softened (half a stick; or
   substitute vegan buttery spread)
2 cups+ confectioners' sugar
3 to 4 tablespoons pumpkin-spice-flavored coffee
   creamer, or as needed (milk, cream, or vegan milk
   may be substituted)
Pumpkin pie spice, for sprinkling

Preheat oven to 375°F. Line a 9 by 9-inch pan with
aluminum foil and spray with cooking spray, or
grease and flour the pan; set aside.

Make the cake. In a large mixing bowl, whisk
together pumpkin, sugars, coconut oil, milk, molasses, vanilla, cinnamon, pumpkin pie spice, allspice,
cloves, nutmeg, and salt, if using, to taste.

Tip: Using room-temperature milk will prevent coconut oil from re-solidifying, but if it does, a few small
white clumps are okay.

Stir in the flour and baking powder until just combined, don't overmix. Batter is quite thick.

Turn batter out into prepared pan, smoothing the
top lightly with a spatula.

Bake for about 27 minutes, or until center is set and
a toothpick inserted in the center comes out clean,
or with a few moist crumbs dangling, but no batter.

Allow cake to cool in pan, on top of a wire rack, for
at least 30 minutes before turning out onto the rack
to finish cooling completely.

While cake cools, make the frosting. In a large
mixing bowl, combine butter, 2 cups confectioners'
sugar, and 3 tablespoons creamer, and beat with an
electric mixer on medium-high speed until smooth.
As needed, drizzle in more creamer until desired
frosting consistency is reached, adjusting the sugar
and creamer ratios slightly and as necessary.

Turn frosting out onto cooled cake, smoothing the
top lightly with a spatula. If you have extra frosting,
it will keep airtight in the refrigerator for at least 3
weeks.

Sprinkle pinches of pumpkin pie spice over the
frosting before slicing and serving. Cake will keep
airtight at room temperature for up to 5 days. I
personally am comfortable storing buttercream-
frosted items at room temperature; if you prefer to
store in the fridge, note that the cake will dry out
more quickly. Unfrosted cake will keep airtight in the
freezer for up to 4 months.

Fudgy Pumpkin Brownies with Fudgy Ganache

"Cakey" isn't a word I ever want associated with brownies, and these brownies are anything but. They're dense, rich, moist, and ultra-fudgy. They're fast and easy to make, coming together in minutes in one bowl, without a mixer. The fudgy ganache is the perfect rich and luxurious complement to these intensely chocolaty brownies. The pumpkin adds plenty of moisture and density, but no dectectable pumpkin flavor. These are intended for serious chocaholics only.

PREP: 15 MINUTES   **BAKE:** 30 MINUTES
TOTAL TIME: ABOUT 75 MINUTES

MAKES ONE 9 BY 9-INCH PAN, 12 GENEROUS AND THICK BROWNIES (SEE NOTE)

Note: Recipe may be baked in a 9 by 13-inch pan for thinner brownies; reduce baking time by 5 to 10 minutes, or as necessary

Brownies

¾ cup unsalted butter (1½ sticks), melted

2 eggs

1 cup granulated sugar

⅔ cup light brown sugar, packed

2 tablespoons coffee or water (leftover coffee from the morning brew is fine)

2 teaspoons vanilla extract

¾ cup pumpkin purée

¾ cup unsweetened dark cocoa powder (unsweetened cocoa powder may be substituted)

1 teaspoon instant espresso granules (make sure to use instant so that it dissolves), optional but recommended

1 cup all-purpose flour

Fudgy Ganache

1½ cups semi-sweet chocolate chips

½ cup half-and-half or cream

Preheat oven to 350°F. Line a 9 by 9-inch baking pan with aluminum foil, and spray with cooking spray; set aside.

Make the brownies. In a large microwave-safe bowl, melt the butter, about 90 seconds on high. Allow the butter to cool momentarily so that the eggs, when added, don't scramble.

Add the eggs, sugars, coffee, and vanilla, and whisk to combine.

Add the pumpkin and whisk to combine.

Add the cocoa powder and instant espresso, and whisk until incorporated, free from lumps, and smooth. This could take a few minutes if your cocoa powder is lumpy.

Add the flour and stir until it's just incorporated; don't overmix.

Turn batter out into prepared pan, smoothing the top lightly with a spatula. Bake for 30 to 34 minutes, or until top has just set, isn't jiggly in the center, and a toothpick inserted in the center comes out clean or with a few fudgy moist crumbs dangling, but no batter; don't overbake. Brownies will firm up more as they cool. Allow brownies to cool in pan.

While brownies cool, make the ganache. Add chocolate chips to a medium, microwave-safe bowl and heat on high for 1 minute to soften chips. They won't be melted; this is okay. Don't stir; set bowl aside.

Heat cream in a glass measuring cup or microwave-safe bowl until it begins to bubble and show signs of just beginning to boil, about 1 minute on high.

Pour cream over chocolate chips and let stand without stirring for 5 to 10 minutes.

Whisk mixture until silky, smooth, and combined. If your mixture isn't smoothing out, heat in 15-second bursts in the microwave until it can be stirred smooth.

Pour ganache over mostly cooled brownies (after about 30 minutes is fine; they don't have to be completely cooled). Smooth ganache lightly with a spatula or offset knife. Cover pan with a sheet of foil (to prevent fridge smells), and place pan in refrigerator until ganache sets up before slicing and serving, at least 2 hours.

Brownies will keep airtight for 1 week at room temperature, for 2 weeks in the refrigerator, and for up to 6 months in the freezer. I highly recommend storing them in the refrigerator—having a slight chill to brownies this rich and fudgy is almost imperative, and it helps to keep the ganache on the fudgier rather than runnier side.

Classic Pumpkin Pie

If you're like most Americans, pumpkin pie is a fixture at the Thanksgiving meal and something you look forward to all year, and this one won't let you down. It has an all-butter, flaky, tender crust. The flavor of butter trumps shortening, and it's an easy crust to make, but if you'd prefer to use a store-bought crust to save time, go for it.

The filling is well spiced and balanced, and comes together with just a whisk in minutes. I tested versions of pie filling using heavy cream, and adding various combinations of sugars and eggs. For ease and without sacrificing any flavor, a can of sweetened condensed milk does the trick. Right along with a couple of tablespoons of bourbon. It won't make the family tipsy sitting around the Thanksgiving table, as much as you may wish it did, because the alcohol burns off while the pie bakes. What remains is lovely depth of flavor—but omit it if you must. Happy Thanksgiving!

PREP: FOR CRUST, 10 MINUTES ACTIVE, BUT ALLOW AT LEAST 1 HOUR FOR CHILLING; UP TO 5 DAYS. FOR FILLING, 5 MINUTES

BAKE: ABOUT 50 MINUTES (NOTE REDUCTION IN OVEN TEMPERATURE AFTER 15 MINUTES)

MAKES ONE 9- OR 10-INCH PIE

Crust

1¼ cups all-purpose flour

1 teaspoon granulated sugar

½ teaspoon salt, or to taste

½ cup cold unsalted butter, cut into small pieces

3 to 4 tablespoons ice water

Tip: To save time, use a prepared 9- or 10-inch piecrust (either refrigerated or frozen; a shelf-stable graham-cracker-crumb crust also works). Keep refrigerated until ready to use. Do not prebake crust before adding the filling. Begin recipe with making the filling.

Filling

15-ounce can pumpkin purée (about 1¾ cups)

14-ounce can sweetened condensed milk

2 eggs

2 tablespoons bourbon, optional but recommended (the alcohol content burns off and the pie will not taste like bourbon, rather it rounds out the flavors and adds depth)

1½ teaspoons cinnamon

1 teaspoon pumpkin pie spice

½ teaspoon allspice

½ teaspoon ground cloves

½ teaspoon ground nutmeg

¼ teaspoon salt

Whipped topping or whipped cream, optional for serving

Prepare the crust. In the canister of a food processor, pulse together flour, sugar, and salt. (Alternatively, use a large mixing bowl and a pastry cutter or two forks.)

Add cold butter and pulse 3 or 4 times until mixture consists of large crumbs; do not overmix at any time.

Tip: One secret to flaky pie crust is visible chunks of butter in the crust mixture; don't be tempted to pulverize them away.

Add the ice water, 1 tablespoon at a time, pulsing 2 or 3 times after each addition until the dough forms into a ball.

Turn the dough out onto plastic wrap and shape it into a flattened mound or disk. Wrap tightly with plastic wrap and refrigerate to chill for at least 1 hour, and up to 5 days.

Tip: Dough may be frozen for up to 3 months before using. Transfer to refrigerator about 24 hours in advance of intended usage.

Prepare a 9- or 10-inch pie dish by spraying with cooking spray; set aside.

On a lightly floured nonstick silicone baking mat or work surface, roll out the dough to about ⅛-inch thick and about 12 inches in diameter, large enough to cover the base and sides of your pie dish.

Gently and carefully drape crust over pie dish and uniformly press it down into the dish. Seal or pinch together any minor cracks or tears caused by transferring.

Crimp the top crust edge with your fingers so that it's flush with the pie-dish edge.

Place crust in refrigerator momentarily while making the filling. Do not prebake this crust before adding the filling.

Tip: The colder you keep the dough before baking, the more it will puff while baking, resulting in flakier crust. Keep the pie dish in the fridge while making the filling.

Make the filling. Preheat oven to 425°F. Combine pumpkin, condensed milk, eggs, bourbon, if using, cinnamon, pumpkin pie spice, allspice, cloves, nutmeg, and salt in a large mixing bowl and whisk together until smooth. Pour into pie crust.

Bake for 15 minutes, reduce oven temperature to 350°F, and bake for about 35 to 40 more minutes (50 to 55 minutes total). A toothpick inserted in the center should come out clean or with just traces of moist crumbs, but no wet batter. If you're an oven-door watcher, at points the filling may puff, dome, and bubble; this is okay; it will shrink and settle as it cools.

Place pie dish on a wire rack and allow to cool completely before serving. Slice and serve as is or with whipped topping or whipped cream.

I prefer my pumpkin pie chilled, so I cover and refrigerate the cooled pie for at least 24 hours before serving it. This also gives the flavors time to marry. Pie will keep airtight in the refrigerator for up to 1 week.

Vanilla-Cream-Cheese-Filled Pumpkin Roll

If you've never made a roll before, don't let that stop you. It looks harder than it really is. The cake is soft, moist, and light. The tangy vanilla-cream-cheese filling is a wonderful complement to the tender cake, which is packed with pumpkin flavor. Set this out at your holiday parties and watch people gravitate toward it. The roll is so eye-catching, and people can't resist the swirl of cream cheese; it just draws them in.

PREP: 20 MINUTES   **BAKE:** 15 MINUTES

MAKES 1 LARGE ROLL, ABOUT 10 1-INCH-THICK SLICES

Cake

¾ cup all-purpose flour

½ teaspoon baking powder

½ teaspoon baking soda

2 teaspoons cinnamon

1 teaspoon pumpkin pie spice

1 teaspoon allspice

½ teaspoon ground cloves

Pinch salt, optional

3 eggs

1 cup granulated sugar

⅔ cup pumpkin purée

2 teaspoons vanilla extract

About ⅓ cup+ confectioners' sugar, for sprinkling on towel (see note)

Note: Have ready a clean, thin kitchen towel similar in size to baking pan (10 by 15 inches), for rolling cake during cooling.

Filling

8 ounces cream cheese, softened

¼ cup unsalted butter (half a stick), softened

2 teaspoons vanilla extract

1½ to 2 cups confectioners' sugar, plus more for dusting if desired

Preheat oven to 350°F. Spray a 10 by 15-inch jelly roll pan (or similarly sized half-sheet pan) with floured cooking spray, or grease and flour the pan; set aside.

Make the cake. In a medium bowl, combine flour, baking powder, baking soda, cinnamon, pumpkin pie spice, allspice, cloves, and salt, if using, to taste, and whisk to combine; set aside.

In the bowl of a stand mixer fitted with the paddle attachment (or use a large mixing bowl and electric hand mixer), beat eggs and granulated sugar on medium-high speed until thick, about 3 minutes.

Add the pumpkin and vanilla, and beat to incorporate.

Add the dry ingredients mixture and beat until just incorporated; don't overmix.

Turn batter out into prepared pan, leaving a 1-inch margin so cake has room to expand while it bakes. Smooth the top lightly with a spatula.

Bake for 13 to 15 minutes, or until cake is set, springy, and a toothpick inserted in center comes out clean.

While cake bakes, lay the kitchen towel on counter or work surface, and generously sprinkle with ⅓+ cup confectioners' sugar (this prevents cake from sticking to towel).

Allow cake to cool in pan for 5 to 10 minutes. Loosen cake with a spatula and carefully turn it out onto prepared towel.

Starting with a short side, roll up the cake and towel together. Place bundle on a wire rack to cool for about 30 minutes.

While the cake cools, make the filling. In the bowl of a stand mixer fitted with the paddle attachment (or use a large mixing bowl with electric hand mixer), beat together cream cheese, butter, and vanilla until fluffy, about 2 minutes.

Stop, scrape down the sides of the bowl, and slowly add 1½ cups confectioners' sugar. Beat until incorporated. Add additional sugar as needed so filling is fairly thick and not runny.

Carefully unroll the cake. Evenly spread filling mixture over cake using a spatula to smooth it. Leave a small bare margin around the edges, about ½ inch.

Re-roll the cake (not with the towel this time). If your cake cracks a bit, it's okay. Many smaller cracks repair themselves while cake is in the fridge or freezer chilling. The filling settles in and absorbs into cracks, so don't worry if yours isn't perfect.

Wrap cake snugly in plastic wrap and refrigerate it for at least 2 hours before slicing, or overnight; or freeze cake for about 1 hour, or until it's very firm but still sliceable. Having it very cold will make slicing easier, less messy, and you'll be able to make thinner slices.

Optionally, dust with confectioners' sugar before slicing and serving. Cake will keep airtight in the refrigerator for up to 5 days.

Pumpkin–Chocolate Chip Bundt Cake with Chocolate Ganache

I have this recipe on my blog, and it's my favorite recipe for pumpkin cake. It's soft, fluffy, and supremely moist. It reminds me of yellow cake-mix cake that's been spiked with pumpkin; it's so springy and tender. It's also a snap to make, coming together with just a whisk and one bowl in minutes. The chocolate chips woven into the batter, combined with the easy, luxurious ganache that drapes the top of the finished cake, makes it taste fancy and rich. It's an excellent cake to serve at parties, and people love it. Only you have to know how easy it is to make.

PREP: 5 MINUTES   **BAKE:** 40 MINUTES

MAKES ONE 12-CUP BUNDT CAKE

Cake

2 eggs

1 cup canned pumpkin purée

1 cup granulated sugar

½ cup canola or vegetable oil

¼ cup sour cream (plain Greek yogurt may be substituted)

1 teaspoon vanilla extract

1 teaspoon butter extract, optional

¼ teaspoon cinnamon

¼ teaspoon pumpkin pie spice

¼ teaspoon allspice

¼ teaspoon cloves

1½ cups all-purpose flour

1 teaspoon baking soda

Pinch salt, optional

1 cup semi-sweet chocolate chips

Chocolate Ganache

MAKES ALMOST 1 CUP, ENOUGH TO GENEROUSLY GLAZE THE CAKE

⅔ cup semi-sweet chocolate chips

¼ cup cream or half-and-half

½ teaspoon vanilla extract

1 to 2 tablespoons rum or bourbon, coffee liqueur, or chocolate-flavored liqueur, optional

Preheat oven to 350°F. Spray a 12-cup bundt or tube-cake pan with floured cooking spray or grease and flour the pan; set aside.

Make the cake. In a large bowl combine eggs, pumpkin, sugar, oil, sour cream, vanilla, butter extract, if using, cinnamon, pumpkin pie spice, allspice, and cloves, and whisk to combine.

Add the flour, baking soda, and salt, if using, and stir until just combined; don't overmix.

Fold in the chocolate chips and pour batter into prepared pan, smoothing it lightly with a spatula.

Give pan a couple of gentle raps on the counter to release air bubbles.

Bake for 38 to 42 minutes, or until top is golden and has set (it may crack; this is okay) and a cake tester, toothpick, or blade of a knife comes out clean, noting that due to the chocolate chips, you may hit some chocolate patches when testing for doneness.

Allow cake to cool in pan for about 15 minutes before inverting and releasing cake from pan. Place cake on a wire rack to cool completely.

While cake cools, make the ganache. In a medium microwave-safe bowl, heat chocolate on high power for 1 minute to soften; set aside.

In a small microwave-safe bowl or measuring cup, heat the cream on high power just until it begins to bubble and show signs of boiling, about 1 minute.

Pour hot cream over chocolate and let it stand about 1 minute. Whisk vigorously until chocolate has melted and mixture is smooth and velvety.

Add vanilla and rum or liqueur, if using and whisk to combine. Set bowl aside for about 5 minutes, allowing ganache to cool and thicken a bit.

Whisk mixture briefly before drizzling it over the cake. Ganache will set up a bit with time, but remains quite viscous and drippy. Cake will keep airtight at room temperature or in the refrigerator for up to 5 days.

Pumpkin-Spice Cupcakes with Marshmallow Buttercream Frosting

Usually I don't need a dozen or two dozen cupcakes; all I really want is one to satisfy my cravings. This is the perfect small-batch cupcake recipe. It's perfect for times when you just want a cupcake or two, and a couple to give to family members, rather than having a dozen or more hanging around to tempt you. Of course if you desire more, double the recipe as necessary. They're soft, fluffy, moist, and light. They're also fast and easy, and you can whip up the batter by hand in less than 5 minutes. My kinda cupcake.

PREP: 10 MINUTES   **BAKE:** ABOUT 18 MINUTES

MAKES 6 CUPCAKES (EASILY DOUBLED IF DESIRED)

Cupcakes

1 egg

¼ heaping cup pumpkin purée

3 tablespoons canola or vegetable oil

2 tablespoons vanilla or plain Greek yogurt
   or sour cream

3 tablespoons granulated sugar

1 tablespoon light brown sugar, packed

1 teaspoon vanilla extract

½ teaspoon cinnamon

¼ teaspoon pumpkin pie spice

¼ teaspoon ground cloves

pinch salt, optional

6 tablespoons all-purpose flour

½ teaspoon baking soda

½ teaspoon baking powder

Marshmallow Buttercream Frosting

MAKES ABOUT 2 CUPS, ENOUGH TO GENEROUSLY FROST THE CUPCAKES

½ cup unsalted butter (1 stick), softened

About ¾ cup marshmallow creme, about half a
   7-ounce jar (see note)

1 teaspoon vanilla extract

1½+ cups confectioners' sugar

Note: Just eyeball it and use half the jar; it's too sticky to measure.

Preheat oven to 350°F and line a standard-sized muffin pan with 6 paper liners or spray with cooking spray; set aside.

Make the cupcakes. In a large mixing bowl combine egg, pumpkin, oil, yogurt, sugars, vanilla, cinnamon, pumpkin pie spice, cloves, and salt, if using, and whisk until smooth and combined.

Add the flour, baking soda, and baking powder, and stir until just incorporated, taking care not to overmix.

Divide batter equally in prepared pan, filling each well between two-thirds and three-quarters full.

Bake for about 18 minutes, or until tops are golden, domed, and set, and a toothpick inserted in the center comes out clean, taking care not to over-bake. Even just 2 extra minutes can result in a much drier cupcake. Allow cupcakes to cool in pan for 5 to 10 minutes before transferring to a rack to finish cooling.

While cupcakes cool, make the frosting. In the bowl of a stand mixer fitted with the paddle attachment (or use a large mixing bowl and hand mixer), beat butter on high speed for 2 to 3 minutes until fluffy.

Stop, scrape down the sides of the bowl, and add the marshmallow creme. Beat on high speed for 2 to 3 minutes, or until fluffy.

Stop, scrape down the sides of the bowl, and add the vanilla and 1½ cups confectioners' sugar, and beat to incorporate, starting slowly and then beating on high speed for about 2 minutes, or until smooth and fluffy.

Depending on desired thickness, add more sugar until desired consistency is reached. If you've added too much sugar and frosting has become too thick, add a dollop of marshmallow creme to thin it back out, or a splash of milk or cream.

Frost cooled cupcakes and serve immediately. Cupcakes are best fresh, but will keep in an airtight container for up to 4 days.

Chocolate-Fudge Pumpkin Poke Cake

This is one of the easiest cakes to make because there are only two ingredients needed to make it: cake mix and pumpkin. That's right—a two-ingredient cake, and it's perfect for feeding a crowd. Cakes similar to this have been around for ages; variations go by the name Better Than . . . Cake. In this version, you simply combine a can of pumpkin purée with chocolate cake mix. No oil, eggs, water, or anything else is added to the batter. After it bakes, you can get your aggression out by poking holes all over your chocolate beauty before flooding her with sweet milk and hot fudge. The whole thing is topped off with creamy whipped topping, making this cake rich, decadent, and a chocolate lover's dream.

PREP: 15 MINUTES **BAKE:** 25 MINUTES
TOTAL TIME: 6+ HOURS, TO ALLOW FOR CHILLING

MAKES ONE 9 BY 13-INCH CAKE, 15 TO 18 GENEROUS PIECES

15- to 16-ounce box devil's food or chocolate cake mix

15-ounce can pumpkin purée

14-ounce can sweetened condensed milk

11- to 12-ounce jar hot fudge sauce, unheated (don't use chocolate syrup, it's too runny)

8-ounce tub whipped topping, thawed (light or fat-free is okay)

About 1 cup mini chocolate chips, or diced peanut butter cups or candy bar, optional, for garnishing

Preheat oven to 350°F. Spray a 9 by 13-inch pan with floured cooking spray or grease and flour the pan; set aside.

In a large bowl, combine the cake mix and pumpkin, and stir until combined. Batter will be fairly thick. Do not add other ingredients called for on the cake mix box such as water, eggs, or oil; just combine cake mix and pumpkin purée.

Bake for about 25 to 28 minutes, or as directed on the cake mix box, or until top is set and springy to the touch. Allow cake to cool for about 10 minutes.

With the blunt (bottom) end of a wooden spoon (perfect size for this job), poke holes all over the cake, about 25 holes; set cake aside.

In small bowl, stir together the sweetened condensed milk and hot fudge sauce. Pour the mixture over the cake, making sure to fill all the holes. It's okay if the liquid pools in places; it will eventually soak in. Allow cake to rest uncovered at room temperature for about 1 hour.

Spread whipped topping over cake, cover, and refrigerate for at least 4 hours, or overnight. If time permits, I strongly recommend overnight chilling to allow the fudge mixture to thoroughly soak in and the flavors to marry.

Prior to serving, optionally garnish with chocolate chips or candies by evenly sprinkling over the top of cake. Cake will keep airtight in the refrigerator for up to 4 days, but may get a little soft from the whipped topping as the days pass.

Flavor Variations

- For more of a cheesecake flavor profile, stir together the whipped topping with 8 ounces of softened cream cheese (light or fat-free is okay) and about 1 cup confectioners' sugar before spreading over cake, and then refrigerate as indicated.
- Try spice cake or yellow cake boxed mixes with 1 teaspoon cinnamon and 1 teaspoon pumpkin pie seasoning stirred in along with the can of pumpkin purée. Replace the jar of hot fudge sauce with a jar of caramel sauce and combine with the sweetened condensed milk as indicated.

Super Moist Pumpkin Cake with Cream Cheese Frosting

This is one supremely moist little cake; hence the title. It's soft, tender, brimming with pumpkin flavor, and did I mention moist? Good thing, because I loathe dry cakes. This one gets rave reviews whenever I serve it, and it's a snap to make. The cream cheese frosting is a must: it is literally the sweet-and-tangy icing on this warmly spiced, springy cake.

PREP: 15 MINUTES **BAKE:** 35 MINUTES

MAKES ONE 8-INCH SQUARE PAN, 9 TO 12 SERVINGS
(SEE NOTE)

Note: The recipe can easily be doubled and baked in a 9 by 13-inch pan. If you're doubling the recipe, use one standard 15-ounce can of pumpkin purée.

Cake

2 eggs

1 cup granulated sugar

1 cup pumpkin purée

½ cup canola or vegetable oil

1 cup all-purpose flour

1 teaspoon baking powder

½ teaspoon baking soda

2 teaspoons ground cinnamon

1 teaspoon pumpkin pie spice

1 teaspoon allspice

Pinch salt, optional

Cream Cheese Frosting

MAKES ABOUT 1½ CUPS, ENOUGH TO FROST THE CAKE

4 ounces cream cheese, softened (light is okay)

¼ cup unsalted butter, softened (half a stick)

1 tablespoon vanilla extract (for maple-flavored frosting, substitute maple extract)

1½ to 2 cups confectioners' sugar, sifted if particularly lumpy (I prefer closer to 2 cups)

Preheat oven to 350°F. Line an 8-inch square pan with foil, leaving overhang, and spray with cooking spray; or grease and flour the pan. Set aside.

Make the cake. In the bowl of a stand mixer fitted with the paddle attachment (or use a large mixing bowl and hand mixer), combine eggs, sugar, pumpkin, and oil, and beat on medium-high speed until smooth, about 3 minutes; set bowl aside.

In a separate large bowl, sift the flour (sifting makes the cake lighter, softer, and fluffier). Add the baking powder, baking soda, spices, and salt, if using, to taste, and stir to combine.

Gradually add the dry mixture to the pumpkin mixture and beat on medium-low speed until combined and smooth, about 2 minutes.

Turn batter out into prepared pan, smoothing top lightly with a spatula. Bake for about 35 minutes, or until center is set and top is springy to the touch. A toothpick inserted in the center should come out

clean, or with a few moist crumbs dangling, but no batter. Allow cake to cool completely in pan on top of a wire rack.

While the cake cools, make the frosting. In the bowl of a stand mixer fitted with the paddle attachment (or use a large mixing bowl and hand mixer), combine cream cheese, butter, and vanilla, and beat on medium-high speed until smooth.

Slowly add the sugar and beat at low speed until frosting is smooth and desired consistency has been reached. Spread frosting evenly over cooled cake.

Using foil overhang, lift cake out of pan, slice, and serve. Cake will keep airtight in the refrigerator (because of the cream cheese frosting) for up to 5 days.

Cheesecake-Topped Pumpkin Cake with Cookies and Caramel Sauce

This is one decadent cake! There are so many layers of flavors and textures going on, including a double dose of pumpkin, in both the cake and cheesecake layers. The cake layer is extremely soft, dense, moist, and tender, courtesy of the buttermilk and pumpkin purée. The luscious layer of pumpkin-flavored cheesecake adds tangy brightness and creaminess. Before serving, crushed gingersnaps are sprinkled over the top, and drizzled caramel sauce glues them in place. The little bits of crunchy ginger cookies are a wonderful contrast to the velvety smooth cheesecake layer. This is a dense, rich, and highly satisfying cake, and despite sounding complicated, it's very fast and easy to make.

CAKE PREP: 10 MINUTES **BAKE:** 30 MINUTES

MAKES ONE 9-INCH CAKE, 8 TO 10 GENEROUS SLICES

6 ounces cream cheese, softened (light is okay)

¼ cup plus ¾ cup pumpkin purée

¼ cup plus ¾ cup granulated sugar

1 teaspoon + 1 teaspoon pumpkin pie spice

1 cup all-purpose flour

½ teaspoon baking powder

½ teaspoon baking soda

1 teaspoon cinnamon

1 teaspoon ground nutmeg

½ teaspoon ground cloves

1 egg, at room temperature

½ cup buttermilk

¼ cup unsalted butter, softened

1½ teaspoons vanilla extract

2 tablespoons turbinado or raw sugar, for sprinkling (granulated may be substituted)

½ cup coarsely crushed gingersnap or speculoos cookies, for sprinkling (cinnamon graham crackers may be substituted)

⅓ cup salted caramel or caramel sauce (see recipe below, or use store-bought), for drizzling

Preheat oven to 375°F. Spray a 9-inch round cake pan or a 9-inch springform pan with floured cooking spray, or grease and flour the pan; set aside.

For the cheesecake layer, combine cream cheese, ¼ cup pumpkin, ¼ cup sugar, and teaspoon of pumpkin pie spice in a small bowl and whisk or use a mixer to beat until smooth and creamy; set bowl aside.

For the cake layer, in the bowl of a stand mixer fitted with the paddle attachment (or use a large mixing bowl and hand mixer), combine ¾ cup sugar, teaspoon pumpkin pie spice, flour, baking powder, baking soda, cinnamon, nutmeg, and cloves, and mix, just to incorporate.

Add the ¾ cup pumpkin, egg, buttermilk, butter, and vanilla, and beat for 1 minute on medium-low speed. Stop, scrape down the sides of the bowl, and beat for 1 minute on medium speed. Turn batter out into prepared pan, smoothing the top lightly with a spatula.

Add the cream cheese mixture in an even layer, spreading and smoothing lightly with a spatula or knife. Sprinkle evenly with turbinado sugar. Bake for 30 minutes, or until center is set and not jiggly, and a toothpick inserted in the center comes out clean, or with a few moist crumbs dangling, but no batter. It's okay if the cheesecake layer is slightly moist in the middle; it's the cake itself to watch and test for doneness.

Allow cake to cool in pan for 10 to 15 minutes before turning out onto a wire rack to cool completely before slicing. If using a regular cake pan and not a springform pan, when inverting, don't be alarmed if the cheesecake layer gets a bit marred. It's going to be covered up with gingersnaps.

Prior to serving cake, sprinkle the gingersnaps evenly over the top of the cake. Drizzle evenly with caramel sauce. Cake will keep airtight in the refrigerator for up to 5 days.

Salted Caramel Sauce

MAKES ABOUT 1 CUP

1 cup granulated sugar

¼ cup water

¾ cup heavy cream

1 tablespoon vanilla extract

¼ cup butter (half a stick; salted or unsalted may be used)

½ to 1 teaspoon kosher salt, or to taste (or omit salt for regular caramel sauce)

In a heavy-bottomed saucepan, combine the sugar and water. Heat over medium-low heat until the sugar dissolves, stirring occasionally.

Increase the heat to medium-high and bring mixture to a boil without stirring. Using caution so as not to burn yourself, use a wet pastry brush or damp paper towel to wipe down any crystals that cling to the sides of the saucepan. Failure to remove them could result in a grainy sauce. Boil until the mixture is a deep amber color, about 5 to 6 minutes.

Remove the pan from the heat, and carefully whisk in the heavy cream. The mixture will bubble up vigorously. Add the vanilla and it will bubble again. Stir in the butter and salt to taste; or omit salt for regular caramel sauce. If using regular table salt rather than kosher salt, add less; it's finer-grained, and 1 teaspoon of table salt is much saltier tasting than 1 teaspoon of kosher salt.

Transfer the caramel to a glass or heatproof jar with a lid. Caramel sauce will keep airtight for months in the refrigerator.

Tip: You can substitute store-bought salted or unsalted caramel sauce for the homemade. Trader Joe's sells Fleur de Sel Salted Caramel Sauce, and Williams-Sonoma carries its own brand.

Pumpkin Carrot Cake with Cream Cheese Frosting

Carrot cake is one of my favorite cakes, and it's even better when infused with pumpkin. The spices used in carrot cake are similar to those in many pumpkin dessert recipes, making the two a natural pairing. The pumpkin flavor is subtle, but incorporating it really helps to keep this cake supremely moist, soft, and springy. My husband and I agree, this is the best carrot cake either of us has ever tasted! This cake is fast and easy to make; the first 12 ingredients are simply whisked together before folding in the rest. As you're savoring bites of soft, tender, texture-loaded cake that's draped in rich and tangy cream cheese frosting, keep telling yourself that you're getting in your required daily servings of vegetables—via cake, which is of course the best way.

PREP: 15 MINUTES **BAKE:** 45 MINUTES

MAKES ONE 9-INCH ROUND IN A SPRINGFORM PAN,
8 TO 10 SERVINGS

Cake

2 eggs

¾ cup granulated sugar

½ cup canola or vegetable oil

½ cup pumpkin purée

¼ cup light brown sugar, packed

¼ cup buttermilk

2 teaspoons ground cinnamon

1 teaspoon pumpkin pie spice

1 teaspoon vanilla extract

½ teaspoon ground cloves

½ teaspoon allspice

½ teaspoon ground nutmeg

1¼ cups all-purpose flour

1 teaspoon baking powder

½ teaspoon baking soda

Pinch salt, optional

1½ cups coarsely grated carrots (see note), measured loosely piled

½ cup raisins, optional

½ cup diced nuts (such as walnuts or pecans), optional

Cream Cheese Frosting

6 ounces cream cheese, softened (light is okay)

¼ cup unsalted butter, softened (half a stick)

**1 tablespoon vanilla extract (for maple-flavored frost-
ing, substitute maple extract)**

**1½ to 2 cups confectioners' sugar, sifted if particu-
larly lumpy (I prefer closer to 2 cups)**

Note: I find grating the carrots by hand, using the
coarsest blade of a box grater, gives superior
results over using a food processor. Please don't
use bagged pre-shredded carrots. You'll likely need
to grate only three carrots, and it takes just a minute to do it by hand—and you'll be much happier
with the results.

Preheat oven to 350°F. Spray a 9-inch springform
pan with floured cooking spray, or grease and flour
the pan; set aside. Do not use a regular 9-inch cake
pan, it's too shallow.

To make the cake, in a large mixing bowl whisk
to combine eggs, granulated sugar, oil, pumpkin,
brown sugar, buttermilk, cinnamon, pumpkin pie
spice, vanilla, cloves, allspice, and nutmeg.

Add the flour, baking powder, baking soda, and
salt, if using, to taste, and fold in until just combined;
don't overmix. Batter will be on the thick side with
some lumps.

Add the carrots, and raisins and nuts, if desired, and
fold to incorporate.

Turn batter out into prepared pan, smoothing top
lightly with a spatula. Bake for 42 to 50 minutes, or
until center is set and top is springy to the touch. A
toothpick inserted in the center should come out
clean, or with a few moist crumbs dangling, but no
batter. Allow cake to cool completely in pan on top
of a wire rack.

While the cake cools, make the frosting. In the bowl
of a stand mixer fitted with the paddle attachment
(or use a large mixing bowl and hand mixer), combine the cream cheese, butter, and vanilla, and beat
on medium-high speed until smooth.

Slowly add the sugar and beat at low speed until
frosting is smooth and desired consistency has
been reached. Spread frosting evenly over cooled
cake, slice, and serve. Store in the refrigerator
(because of the cream cheese frosting) airtight, for
up to 5 days.

Bourbon Pumpkin Ice Cream with Chocolate Cookies and Chunks

This is some of the best ice cream I've ever had, and it's the easiest to make, with just two main ingredients—whipped cream and sweetened condensed milk. It calls for only one bowl, and it's a no-cook recipe, so there are no eggs to cook, no sugar to stir in, no waiting for a hot mixture to cool down. An added plus: you don't need an ice-cream maker to make it, although instructions are included below if you have one and want to use it.

The ice cream is ridiculously rich, creamy, and decadent. It's infused with pumpkin and spices, and has an understated note of smooth bourbon. The chocolate chunks and cookies add texture and pizzazz to this pants-size-enhancing blend.

PREP: 10 MINUTES   **TOTAL:** 6 HOURS FOR CHILLING

MAKES ABOUT 2 QUARTS (64 OUNCES)

2 cups heavy whipping cream (if using an ice-cream maker, use 4 cups [1 quart])

14-ounce can sweetened condensed milk

3 tablespoons bourbon (omit if you must, but highly recommended)

1 tablespoon vanilla extract

24 chocolate-flavored sandwich cookies, such as Oreos, coarsely chopped

8 to 10 ounces semi-sweet or dark chocolate, medium-coarsely chopped

¼ cup pumpkin purée

2 tablespoons pumpkin pie spice

In the bowl of a stand mixer fitted with the whisk attachment (or use a large mixing bowl and hand mixer), whip 2 cups heavy cream to very stiff peaks, about 5 minutes on high power.

Add half the can of sweetened condensed milk, bourbon, and vanilla, and fold gently to combine. After the mixture is combined, add the remaining sweet milk. "Fold" means turn the mixture over with a spatula from the bottom of the bowl up, rotate the bowl, and repeat until the mixture is homogenous. The goal is to keep all that fluffy cream you just made as fluffy as possible. Take your time and be gentle. If the mixture has deflated or is on the soupy side, turn the mixer back on, and whip for another few minutes until it's re-puffed.

Add the cookies, chocolate, pumpkin, and pumpkin pie spice, and fold gently to combine.

Transfer ice cream mixture to a freezer-safe 2-quart container with a lid or freezer-safe bowl that can be covered with plastic wrap.

Cover and freeze for at least 6 hours, or until solid. Before serving, allow ice cream to sit out about 5 minutes at room temperature. Ice cream will keep airtight in the freezer for up to 3 months.

Ice-Cream Maker Method

Stir together 4 cups heavy cream, sweetened condensed milk, bourbon, and vanilla.

Stir in cookies, chocolate, pumpkin, and pumpkin pie spice.

Follow processing directions on ice-cream maker, noting to chill the mixture if necessary before churning.

Savory:
Sides, Soups, and
Starters

Soft Buttery Pumpkin Pretzels

If you struggle with willpower, one of the most dangerous places to be is the food court at the mall. Everywhere you turn, there's something tempting—fresh chocolate chip cookies, big cinnamon rolls, and soft, buttery pretzels. Now you don't have to go to the mall to be tempted. You can make your own mall-style soft pretzels at home.

This is an easy yeast dough that's a dream to work with—smooth, supple, and not at all sticky. I eliminated the step of boiling the pretzels before baking to streamline things for newer bread makers, and built in a make-ahead option in case you want to start the dough one day and bake pretzels the next.

The pumpkin serves to keep the pretzels soft, moist, and tender. It lends a vibrant shade of orange to the dough rather than imparting much flavor. Think of it as a way to work in some vegetables—or fruit, technically—along with the carbs. You'll thank me later that I capped the batch size at six, because these pretzels are irresistible. Serve them as is or with your favorite dips or condiments. Or get creative and take them in a different direction, sweet or savory (see Variations).

PREP: 20 MINUTES   **BAKE:** 10 MINUTES
TOTAL: ABOUT 4 HOURS, MOSTLY DOWNTIME FOR DOUGH RISING

MAKES 6 LARGE PRETZELS

½ cup milk for dissolving yeast

1 teaspoon granulated sugar

¼-ounce packet instant dry yeast (2¼ teaspoons)

1 egg

½ cup pumpkin purée

2 tablespoons canola or vegetable oil, or melted butter

1 teaspoon salt

2½ cups all-purpose flour (see note), plus more for flouring work surface

¼ cup+ melted salted or unsalted butter for brushing, divided

Kosher or sea salt for sprinkling, to taste

Note: Bread flour may be substituted; it will produce a higher-rising dough and chewier pretzels. If using bread flour, you may need slightly less than if using all-purpose. All-purpose creates softer, more tender pretzels, and that's what I prefer.

Heat the milk according to temperature indicated on package for yeast you're using (temps will likely range from 100°F to 130°F, depending on brand; about 30 to 45 seconds in the microwave). In the bowl of a stand mixer (or use a large mixing bowl and wooden spoon), combine the warm milk and sugar, and sprinkle the yeast over it. Allow it to proof, getting bubbly and foamy, about 5 minutes.

Add the egg, pumpkin, oil, and salt, and mix briefly with the paddle attachment on low speed to combine, about 1 minute.

Add 2½ cups flour and switch to the dough hook when dough comes together and can be kneaded (or knead by hand). Knead for about 5 to 7 minutes, or until smooth and elastic; this is not a sticky dough and should be smooth.

Turn dough out into a large mixing bowl coated with cooking spray, turning dough over once to grease the top.

Cover with plastic wrap and place in a warm, draft-free place to rise until doubled in bulk, about 2½ to 3 hours.

Tip: To use your oven as a warm, draft-free rising place for dough, see Tips and Tricks, no. 3, page xvi.

Prepare two baking sheets by lining them with non-stick baking mats or spraying with cooking spray; set aside.

Punch dough down; turn out onto a lightly floured surface (I use a nonstick baking mat and don't need any flour).

Divide into 6 equally sized portions.

With your hands, roll each portion of dough into a long, thin rope, 24 to 28 inches long, and twist each rope into a pretzel. When forming the pretzels, I envision making a heart, with a twist in the middle, and drape the ends loosely over the opposite side.

Place three pretzels on each of the two prepared baking sheets. Cover with plastic wrap and allow pretzels to rise in a warm, draft-free place until nearly doubled, about 1 hour.

In the final minutes of rising, preheat oven to 350°F. (If using the oven as a rising place, make sure to remove pretzels from oven before you preheat.)

Before baking, liberally brush pretzels with melted butter; reserve remainder.

Bake for 10 to 12 minutes, or until they're golden, puffed, and done. I prefer softer pretzels and bake for 10 minutes; for firmer pretzels bake longer.

After baking, immediately brush pretzels with reserved melted butter. Sprinkle with kosher salt.

Serve immediately, either as is or with mustard (Dijon, hot, honey, spicy), horseradish, cream cheese, or hummus (for Pumpkin Chipotle Hummus, see page 98). Pretzels are best warm and fresh, but will keep airtight for up to 48 hours. I quickly zap them in the microwave before eating leftovers.

Tip: For a make-ahead option, after the first rise and punch-down, form a ball with the dough, wrap it in plastic wrap, and refrigerate for up to 48 hours. When ready to bake, pick up the recipe starting with rolling the dough into long ropes, and continue from there.

Variations

- Boost the pumpkin flavor by sprinkling with pumpkin pie spice after baking.

- For cinnamon-sugar pretzels, omit the kosher salt finishing sprinkle and dredge freshly baked and buttered pretzels in a cinnamon-sugar mixture.

- Play up the savory element by brushing with garlic butter or herbed butter.

Smoky Roasted Vegetable and Peanut Soup

This soup is layered with so many rich and comforting flavors, including smoky roasted carrots, red peppers, and pumpkin. Roasting the vegetables before blending them lends so much depth of flavor to this vegan, gluten-free, very fast and easy soup. Coconut milk is used in place of soup stock and adds creaminess and richness, and balances the smokiness from the roasted veggies. The soup is hearty, healthy, satisfying, and warms you right up.

PREP: 15 MINUTES **ROAST:** 40 MINUTES
COOK: 10 MINUTES

MAKES ABOUT 5 CUPS THICK, HEARTY SOUP

1 pound carrots plus (for roasting; set aside
   1 tablespoon shredded, for garnishing)
1 very large or 2 medium red bell peppers
   (for roasting; set aside 1 tablespoon diced,
   for garnishing)
2 tablespoons olive oil
1 teaspoon salt
½ teaspoon black pepper
14-ounce can coconut milk (light is okay)
½ cup pumpkin purée
¼ cup creamy peanut butter
1 to 2 tablespoons agave, maple syrup, or honey,
   optional
Salt and pepper, for seasoning soup
Pinch of red pepper flakes, cayenne pepper,
   or chili powder, optional
Sour cream, for garnishing
Peanuts, chopped, for garnishing

Preheat oven to 400°F. Prepare two baking sheets by lining them with nonstick baking sheets, parchment paper, or aluminum foil, or spraying sheets with cooking spray; set aside.

Peel and chop the carrots into about 1½-inch chunks, keeping them approximately the same size so they cook evenly; place carrots on one baking sheet.

Deseed and quarter the pepper, or slice it into five or six large wedges. Peppers must be kept much larger than the carrots, because they will shrink in size by nearly half when roasted, and if sliced too small to begin with, they'll char.

Place pepper slices on the other baking sheet. Evenly drizzle olive oil over top of vegetables and sprinkle them with salt and pepper.

Roast vegetables for about 40 minutes, or until carrots are fork-tender and have browned and caramelized; peppers will be soft, limp, and blackened around the edges. Flip the vegetables midway through cooking if desired (I don't bother).

In the canister of a high-speed blender or food processor, combine coconut milk, pumpkin, roasted vegetables, and peanut butter, and blend until desired texture is reached.

The soup will be quite thick; if desired, it may be thinned with additional coconut milk, vegetable stock, or a splash of water.

Taste the soup and, if desired, sweeten it with agave, maple syrup, or honey to balance the smokiness. Season to taste with salt and pepper. If you prefer spicier soup, a pinch of red pepper flakes, cayenne pepper, or chili powder kicks up the heat.

Before serving, garnish with a dollop of sour cream and finely diced red peppers, grated carrots, and a sprinkle of peanuts.

Soup will keep airtight for up to 5 days in the refrigerator or in the freezer for up to 3 months.

Parmesan and Cream Cheese Pumpkin Puffs

If you've never worked with puff pastry, you're going to love how versatile it is. I make everything from chocolate turnovers to cinnamon rolls to cheesy puffs with it. Although I have a huge sweet tooth, cheese does make everything taste so good. These little puffs are filled with two kinds of cheese, and they're a cinch to make. They're a perfect vegetarian party appetizer because they're so fast and easy. Or, grab a handful and make a meal out of them.

PREP: 10 MINUTES   **BAKE:** 20 MINUTES

MAKES 1 DOZEN PUFFS

⅔ cup pumpkin purée

½ cup cream cheese, softened (fat-free or light
   is okay)

1 sheet puff pastry, thawed but still cold (see note)

1 heaping tablespoon all-purpose seasoning blend
   (like Lawry's, Grill Mates, Mrs. Dash)

Salt and pepper, optional

½ cup grated Parmesan cheese

1 egg

1 tablespoon water

Note: Puff pastry is commonly sold in a 17.2-ounce box with 2 sheets per box; for this recipe, you need 1 sheet, which measures about 8 inches square.

Tip: With the leftover sheet of puff pastry, make PB&J Pinwheels—kids love them. Spread pastry with about ⅓ cup peanut butter, ¼ cup jelly, roll up into a log, slice, and bake. Or use Nutella. You can also make cinnamon rolls by spreading about ¼ cup softened butter on the pastry. Sprinkle heavily with cinnamon and granulated or brown sugar, roll up, slice, and bake.

Preheat oven to 400°F. Spray a 12-cup standard muffin pan with cooking spray, making sure to spray thoroughly to prevent the puffs from sticking; set aside.

In a medium bowl, stir together the pumpkin purée and cream cheese. Some small cream cheese chunks are okay; set aside.

Unwrap puff pastry and place on a clean, lightly floured counter or work surface.

Spread pumpkin and cream cheese mixture over the puff pastry, leaving a half-inch margin on all sides.

Sprinkle seasoning blend evenly over the top.

Sprinkle with salt and pepper, if using, to taste. (Take care not to oversalt: some seasoning blends are already heavily salted, and both the cream cheese and Parmesan cheese have salt.)

Evenly sprinkle Parmesan cheese over the top.

Roll up the puff pastry in as tightly wound cylinder (log) as possible.

With a very sharp knife or bench scraper, slice the log into 12 equal-sized pieces. This is messy; some filling will leak out, the slices will seem very thin and skimpy—all normal and okay. Just get them into the pan any way you can, pretty or not. Place one slice in each well of the prepared pan; set aside.

In a small bowl, lightly beat together the egg and water to create an eggwash. Brush eggwash over pastry slices, distributed evenly until it's gone.

Bake for about 20 minutes, or until puffs are golden, puffed, set, and done. The cheese and egg will be glistening and a bit bubbly.

Allow puffs to cool in pan for about 5 minutes before removing. Wedge the tip of a rubber spatula into the pan to "pop" them out if they're being stubborn. Serve immediately. Extra puffs will keep airtight in the refrigerator for up to three days; reheat gently in the microwave before serving.

These are delicious as is, but you can also serve them with mustard, horseradish, ranch dressing, or ketchup (especially for kids—everything is better with ketchup).

Pumpkin-Spice Candied Nuts

Going to the mall before the holidays is not always fun or easy. The crowds, the parking hassles, harried shoppers stressing out and melting down. Thank goodness for the smell of candied nuts wafting in the air. In case you want to just skip the mall and eat mall-style candied nuts at home, this is your chance. Although there's some heat from the cayenne, they're not overly hot or spicy. But if you're not a fan of heat or are making these for others who aren't, you can reduce or omit it. The nuts make great gifts, but they may not last long enough to give away. They're addictively crunchy, and once you grab a handful, you'll need at least five more.

PREP: 5 MINUTES **BAKE:** 28–30 MINUTES

MAKES ABOUT 4 CUPS

3 cups nuts (see note)

1 egg white

1 tablespoon water

⅔ cup granulated sugar

⅓ cup brown sugar, packed (light or dark)

2 teaspoons pumpkin pie spice

2 teaspoons cinnamon

1 teaspoon kosher salt

½ teaspoon cayenne pepper (reduce to ¼ teaspoon for milder heat)

Note: Pecans work very well to absorb the coating. I like a mixture of 1 cup each of pecans, walnuts, and almonds. I use raw and unsalted nuts; roasted, lightly salted nuts can also be used.

Preheat oven to 300°F. Line a baking sheet with parchment paper; set aside.

In a large bowl, combine the nuts; set aside.

In a small bowl, whisk together the egg white and water until frothy, foamy, and bubbly, about 2 minutes by hand. Pour mixture over nuts and toss to coat evenly; set aside.

In a medium bowl, whisk together the sugars, pumpkin pie spice, cinnamon, salt, and cayenne pepper. Pour over the nuts and toss to coat evenly.

Turn nuts out onto prepared baking sheet, spreading them in a flat, even layer.

Bake for 28 to 30 minutes, stirring once midway through cooking. Remove from oven, lift the parchment paper with the nuts on it off the baking tray, set it on the counter, and allow nuts to cool.

When nuts are cool enough to handle, break apart any large nut clusters, as desired.

Transfer nuts to airtight containers or jars. Nuts will keep airtight at room temperature for at least 1 month.

Pumpkin Chipotle Hummus

I love dips and spreads of any kind, especially hummus, and it's one of the easiest and fastest things to make at home. After trying fresh, homemade hummus that can be customized with your preferred spices and seasonings, it's difficult to go back to store-bought. And think of all the money you'll save—those little store-bought containers of hummus are pricey, and there's not much in them. This recipe makes a nice big batch, perfect for those of us who can make a meal out of chips and dip.

PREP: 5 MINUTES

MAKES 2 HEAPING CUPS

15-ounce can garbanzo beans (chickpeas), drained and rinsed

1 cup pumpkin purée

2 to 3 tablespoons olive oil, plus more for drizzling before serving

1 tablespoon+ chipotle seasoning blend (see note)

½ teaspoon+ salt

Note: Because seasonings vary widely by type and brand, adjust measurement to taste.

Combine beans, pumpkin, oil, chipotle seasoning, and salt in a blender or food processor and process on high speed until smooth; or, if chunkier hummus is preferred, blend or pulse in short bursts until desired consistency is reached.

Before serving with your favorite chips, crackers, bread, or vegetables, drizzle with olive oil, if desired. Hummus will keep airtight for up to 5 days in the refrigerator.

Honey-Butter Pumpkin Dinner Rolls

These rolls are soft and slightly chewy, and the pumpkin purée keeps them moist and adds just the right amount of tooth-sinking density. The pumpkin flavor is present, but not so much as to compete with the other foods on your dinner plate. This is a fast yeast recipe because the dough rises like a champ; from start to finish, the rolls are ready in about two hours. It's a smooth, easy dough to work with and not at all sticky. The recipe makes a modest batch of rolls, nice for singles or small families, and extras freeze beautifully. I've also included a make-ahead option.

PREP: 15 MINUTES   **BAKE:** 16 MINUTES
TOTAL TIME: ABOUT 2 HOURS, MOSTLY DOWNTIME FOR RISING

MAKES 8 TO 10 HEARTY ROLLS

Rolls

⅓ cup milk

2 tablespoons unsalted butter

1 egg

½ cup pumpkin purée

2¼ cups all-purpose flour (see note)

¼-ounce packet instant dry yeast (2¼ teaspoons)

1 tablespoon granulated sugar

1 tablespoon pumpkin pie spice

1 teaspoon ground nutmeg

½ teaspoon salt, optional

Note: Bread flour may be substituted; rolls will be firmer and chewier rather than softer and fluffier; you may only need 2 cups bread flour.

Honey Butter

2 tablespoons unsalted butter, melted

2 tablespoons honey

Make the rolls. In a 2-cup microwave-safe measuring cup or a microwave-safe bowl, combine milk and butter and heat on high power, about 45 seconds. Stir until butter has melted smoothly into the milk.

Add the egg and pumpkin, and whisk to combine.

Return measuring cup to microwave and heat for about 15 seconds to warm mixture up. This helps to activate the yeast; set aside briefly.

In the bowl of a stand mixer fitted with the dough hook (or a large mixing bowl if kneading by hand), combine the flour, yeast, sugar, pumpkin pie spice, nutmeg, and salt, if using, to taste.

Pour wet pumpkin mixture over the dry ingredients.

Turn mixer to low speed, and knead for 5 to 8 minutes, or until dough is smooth and has come together. If kneading by hand, turn dough out onto a clean, lightly floured work surface and knead for about 10 minutes, or until dough is soft, smooth, and has come together. This is not a sticky dough; if your dough is sticky, tacky, or gloppy, add additional flour, 1 tablespoon at a time, until dough is no longer sticky. Take care not to overflour the dough; over-flouring makes for dense and heavy rolls.

Turn dough out into a mixing bowl that's been lightly sprayed with cooking spray. Flip dough over once so both sides are lightly greased, and cover bowl with plastic wrap.

Place bowl in a warm, draft-free environment until dough has nearly doubled in bulk, about 45 to 60 minutes. Wait until dough has nearly doubled in size; if it takes longer than an hour, that's fine.

Tip: To use your oven as a warm, draft-free rising place for dough, see Tips and Tricks, no. 3, page xvi.

Prepare a 9-inch square pan by lining with foil and spraying with cooking spray; set aside.

Punch dough down and turn it out onto a nonstick surface. (I spray my counter with cooking spray and don't even add flour.)

Divide dough into 8 to 12 equally sized portions, rolling each portion into a ball. You can make eight very generously sized rolls; I suggest making nine to ten. They may look skimpy now but they rise and swell very nicely.

Place dough balls into prepared pan. .

Cover pan with a sheet of foil and place pan in a warm, draft-free environment until dough has nearly doubled in bulk, about 45 minutes.

In the last minutes of rising, preheat oven to 375°F.

While the oven preheats, make the honey butter. Melt butter in small microwave-safe bowl, about 45 seconds on high power.

Add the honey and stir to combine.

Before baking, generously brush dough with honey-butter mixture; reserve any extra and brush it on after baking.

Bake for 15 to 17 minutes, or until rolls are puffed, golden, domed, and cooked through; when tapped, the rolls should sound hollow. Allow rolls to cool in pan until they're cool enough to handle before serving. Rolls will keep airtight at room temperature for up to 4 days. Heat in microwave for 5 to 10 seconds as necessary to re-create the just-baked taste and to soften. Finished (baked) rolls will keep airtight in the freezer for up to 6 months.

Tip: For an overnight or make-ahead option, after putting dough balls in pan and before the second rise, cover with foil and refrigerate. When ready to bake, transfer pan to a warm, draft-free place until dough doubles in size (this could take an hour or so, since dough is coming out of a cold fridge). Resume recipe with making the honey butter.

Bourbon Maple Slow-Cooker Baked Beans

These are the best baked beans I've ever had, and the recipe is nearly work-free. Although most baked bean recipes start out with bacon and pork fat, this recipe is vegan and gluten-free. You won't lose one ounce of flavor or miss the fat.

If you've never made beans in a slow cooker, it's so easy. You do have to have some patience, because they cook for at least 12 hours, but the best things come to those who wait, right? The flavors of bourbon, maple syrup, brown sugar, molasses, barbecue sauce, and pumpkin intensify and concentrate over time, and the resulting beans have incredible depth of flavor. They're sweet with a bit of heat, robust yet smooth, and extremely satisfying.

To keep vegan and gluten-free, take care that all ingredients used are suitable for your dietary needs, reading labels and selecting specific brands as necessary.

PREP AND ACTIVE WORK: 15 MINUTES
TOTAL TIME: 12 TO 16 HOURS

MAKES ABOUT 8 CUPS

1 pound dry great northern beans (or navy beans)
1 cup bourbon
1 cup maple syrup
1 cup barbecue sauce
1 cup light brown sugar, packed
1 cup water
¼ cup pumpkin purée
¼ cup ketchup
¼ cup mustard (I use yellow, if using stoneground or dijon, consider using slightly less)
¼ cup light, mild, or medium molasses (not blackstrap)
¼ cup olive oil
¼ cup apple cider vinegar
2 tablespoons Worcestershire sauce (to keep vegan, use vegan Worcestershire)

Sort and rinse dry beans. In a large pot, cover beans with 8 cups water. Let soak overnight (about 8 hours).

Tip: To save time, use the 1-hour rapid-soak method. Bring beans and 8 cups water to a boil. Allow beans to boil rapidly for 3 minutes, uncovered. Shut the heat off, cover the pot, and let stand for 1 hour.

Drain beans and rinse well under running water.

Return beans to pot, cover with 6 cups water, and allow to simmer on low heat for about 45 minutes, or until somewhat tender. The beans won't be done, but they shouldn't be overly hard either (cooked about 80 percent through; taste to check).

While beans are simmering, combine bourbon, maple syrup, barbecue sauce, brown sugar, water, pumpkin, ketchup, mustard, molasses, oil, vinegar, and Worcestershire sauce in slow cooker, and whisk until smooth.

Drain beans, add to slow cooker, and stir to combine.

Cover and cook on low heat for about 12 hours (start checking at about 8 hours), or until beans are tender, the sauce has thickened and reduced dramatically, the flavor is concentrated and robust, and the smell in your house is intoxicating.

If after 12 hours your sauce is still on the thin or soupy side, remove the lid, increase the heat to the highest setting, and cook uncovered until thickened to desired level.

Note: Because slow-cookers vary greatly, you may need to tinker with the temperature settings in cooking beans. You might cook on medium for 10 to 12 hours, or on high for 8 to 10 hours, or use a combination of settings until your sauce has thickened and the beans are tender.

Serve immediately. Beans will keep airtight in the refrigerator for up to one week, and taste better on days two and three as the flavors marry even more. Finished beans can be frozen for up to six months.

Sweet Potato and Pumpkin Coconut-Milk Soup

This is the fastest and easiest soup I make, and one of the most flavorful, rich, and hearty. It's also vegan, gluten-free, and a healthful meal that I feel good about serving to my family. The sweet potatoes are steamed in the microwave and then blended with red peppers, pumpkin, and coconut milk. This soup goes from pantry to table in about 15 minutes, making it a great choice when you want warm, homemade soup without any of the fuss of turning on the stove or oven.

PREP: 5 MINUTES   **COOK:** 13 MINUTES

MAKES ABOUT 4½ CUPS THICK, HEARTY SOUP

1 extra-large sweet potato (or 2 to 3 smaller sweet potatoes), peeled and diced into 1-inch cubes

About ¾ cup water

1 large red bell pepper, de-seeded and chopped into large pieces (optionally, reserve about 1 tablespoon diced for garnishing)

14-ounce can coconut milk (light is okay)

½ cup pumpkin purée

1 teaspoon pumpkin pie spice

½ teaspoon red pepper flakes, optional

Salt and pepper

Sour cream, for garnishing

Put sweet potato cubes in a large microwave-safe bowl, and add about ¾ cup water, or fill until about an inch of water covers the base of the bowl. The cubes do not need to be fully submerged; water simply needs to be present to create steam.

Cover bowl with plastic wrap, and heat on high for 13 to 15 minutes, or until sweet potatoes are very fork-tender. Microwave temperatures and strengths vary and so will cooking times.

Drain the water and transfer cooked potatoes to a high-speed blender or food processor.

Add the bell pepper, coconut milk, pumpkin, pumpkin pie spice, red pepper flakes, if using, and salt and pepper to taste, and blend on high power until desired texture is reached.

Before serving, optionally garnish with a dollop of sour cream and finely diced red peppers.

Soup will keep airtight for up to 5 days in the refrigerator or in the freezer for up to 3 months.

Honey-Maple Pumpkin Beer Bread

This bread is so simple to make, you'll think you're doing something wrong. It's some of the best, and definitely the easiest, bread I make. No-knead, no fuss, foolproof, and goofproof. The yeast for the bread comes via one bottle of beer, and you just pour the beer over everything that's in your bowl, stir, and bake. In case you're not a beer fan, not to worry—the bread doesn't taste like beer. The beer helps give it an amazingly soft, springy, bouncy texture. The bread is perfect for making into French toast, bread pudding, or for sandwiches. Serve it with soup, chili, dip it in hummus or oil and balsamic, or just add a smear of butter.

PREP: 5 MINUTES   **COOK:** 40 MINUTES
TOTAL: ABOUT 1 HOUR, TO ALLOW FOR COOLING

MAKES 1 TALL 9 BY 5 LOAF, ABOUT 12 THICK SLICES

2 tablespoons canola or vegetable oil

2 tablespoons light, mild, or medium molasses (not blackstrap)

¼ cup honey

¼ cup maple syrup

2 tablespoons pumpkin purée

1 teaspoon pumpkin pie spice

1 teaspoon cinnamon

1 teaspoon ground nutmeg

½ teaspoon salt, optional

3 cups all-purpose flour

1 tablespoon baking powder

12 ounces pumpkin beer (or use your favorite beer)

Preheat oven to 375°F. Spray a 9 by 5-inch loaf pan with floured cooking spray, or grease and flour the pan; set aside.

In a large mixing bowl, add oil, molasses, honey, maple syrup, pumpkin, pumpkin pie spice, cinnamon, nutmeg, salt (if using) to taste, flour, and baking powder, and whisk to combine.

Tip: Measure the oil, molasses, honey, and maple syrup using the same ¼-cup measure. The oil coats the measuring cup, enabling the subsequent ingredients to slide right out. (Note that there are 4 tablespoons in ¼ cup, so filling it halfway gives you 2 tablespoons.)

Slowly pour beer over the top of bread mixture. It will bubble and foam. Stir until combined. Batter will be thick, gloppy, and dense.

Turn batter out into prepared pan, smoothing the top lightly with a spatula. Bake for about 40 to 43 minutes, or until top is domed and set, and a toothpick inserted in the center comes out clean or with a few moist crumbs dangling, but no batter.

Allow bread to cool in pan for about 15 minutes before turning out onto a wire rack to cool completely. Slice using a serrated knife. Bread is best fresh, but will keep airtight for up to 4 days. As the days pass, toasting it is recommended; or make croutons with it.

Variations

For a more savory flavor, omit the honey, pumpkin pie spice, cinnamon, and nutmeg, and add garlic or onion powder, curry, oregano, dill, or your favorite spice blend. Or, for a cheesy beer bread, add a handful of shredded cheese to the batter.

Cheesy Baked Pumpkin Mac 'n' Cheese

Growing up, I actually preferred the mac 'n' cheese that comes in a box with the packet of electric-orange-colored powder. Now my tastes are somewhat more refined, as this recipe reflects. The pumpkin flavor is subtle and doesn't distract from the creamy, cheesy noodles that lay beneath a slightly crunchy baked-breadcrumb topping. This mac 'n' cheese is hearty, filling, and rich—unabashed comfort food at its finest.

For a stove-top-only version, omit the bread-crumb topping and serve mac 'n' cheese directly from the pan, after tossing pasta with the cheese sauce. You can also make the baked dish ahead of time (see Tip).

PREP: 20 MINUTES **BAKE:** 35 MINUTES

MAKES ONE 8-INCH SQUARE PAN, 4 TO 6 SERVINGS (RECIPE IS EASILY DOUBLED AND BAKED IN A 9 BY 13-INCH PAN)

Mac 'n' Cheese

8 ounces rigatoni or elbow macaroni (half a 1-pound box), dry

2 tablespoons unsalted butter, melted

2 tablespoons all-purpose flour

1¼ cups half-and-half (or cream or milk)

½ cup pumpkin purée

¾ teaspoon dry ground yellow mustard

¾ teaspoon paprika

½ teaspoon ground nutmeg

¼ teaspoon salt

¼ teaspoon black pepper

8 ounces (about 2 cups) extra-sharp cheddar cheese, grated; divided

4 ounces (about 1 cup) grated Parmesan and Pecorino Romano cheese blend, or similar

Breadcrumb Topping

¼ cup (half a stick) unsalted butter

¾ cup bread crumbs or panko

1 teaspoon paprika

This is a fast-moving recipe when making the cheese sauce. Make sure you have all ingredients in place and have read the recipe in its entirety before beginning.

Line an 8-inch square pan with aluminum foil and spray with cooking spray, or use a similar-sized oven-safe baking dish sprayed with cooking spray; set aside.

Cook macaroni according to package directions for firm, or al dente, pasta. (Don't overcook. When baked, macaroni will turn to mush if overcooked at this point.) Drain, rinse, and set aside.

Make the cheese sauce. In a large pot, melt 2 table-spoons butter over low heat.

Stir in flour to make a roux. Cook for about 1 minute, stirring constantly. Remove from heat.

Stir in the half-and-half, return pan to the heat, and cook over medium-low until mixture begins to simmer. Cook for 1 minute to thicken, stirring constantly.

Stir in pumpkin, mustard, paprika, nutmeg, and salt and pepper to taste.

Stir in about 1½ cups cheddar, plus all the Parmesan and Pecorino Romano, and cook over medium-low until cheese is melted, about 1 minute, stirring nearly constantly. Turn off the heat.

Add the pasta and toss to coat.

Preheat oven to 350°F.

Transfer mac 'n' cheese to prepared pan. Sprinkle remaining ½ cup cheddar cheese evenly over the top; set pan aside.

Make the topping. In a medium microwave-safe bowl, melt the butter (about 45 seconds on high). Add breadcrumbs and lightly stir or toss with a fork until small clumps form.

Evenly sprinkle breadcrumbs over the cheese. Sprinkle with 1 teaspoon paprika.

Bake for about 35 minutes, or until golden. Serve immediately. Mac 'n' cheese can be stored airtight in the refrigerator for up to 5 days and reheated gently in the microwave prior to serving.

Tip: For a make-ahead option, this dish can be prepared and kept covered in the refrigerator for up to 48 hours before baking. This is great if you're having a party or event, or just want to get a jumpstart on the week's meals.

Maple-Pumpkin Broiled Tofu

This tofu will make a believer out of people who insist they don't like tofu. It's firm, chewy, and full of intense, bold flavors from the pumpkin, maple syrup, and ginger. Cayenne pepper lends a kick and makes it addictive in the way spicier foods are—once you start, you want more.

The secret to making restaurant-style tofu at home is to use extra-firm tofu that's been very well pressed to remove the water. I love tofu but cannot stand it if it's mushy. Removing the water before marinating it is key to creating dense and chewy tofu. After a quick stint under the broiler, the tofu is ready in minutes; the marinade thickens, caramelizes, and takes on a smoky flavor, almost like it's been barbecued. It's vegan, gluten-free, good for you, and delicious!

PREP: 10 MINUTES   **BROIL:** ABOUT 9 MINUTES
TOTAL: 90 MINUTES+ WITH PRESSING AND MARINATING

MAKES 12 TO 16 THIN SLICES

16-ounce block extra-firm tofu

Heaping ½ cup pumpkin purée

½ cup maple syrup

1 heaping teaspoon ground ginger

1 teaspoon dry ground yellow mustard

1 teaspoon ground nutmeg

½ teaspoon ground cloves

¼ teaspoon cayenne pepper (for spicier tofu, use ½ teaspoon)

Salt and pepper

Open tofu package, drain the water, and press the tofu in a tofu press for at least one hour or overnight; refrigerate it if you're pressing overnight.

Tip: If you don't have a tofu press, roll the block of tofu in at least eight paper towels, wrapping it snugly round and round. Put the wrapped tofu on a rimmed baking sheet, and top it with another baking sheet. Put something heavy, like a cookbook or bag of sugar, on top of that. The weight of the heavy object will cause the tofu to release water and the paper towels will soak it up; excess water will be contained in the baking sheet. If the paper towels become drenched, unbundle and rewrap as necessary. The most water will be released in the first 30 minutes, but there is value to pressing tofu for up to 24 hours for that extra, extra-chewy quality. If you plan to press it for longer than 3 or 4 hours, refrigerate it.

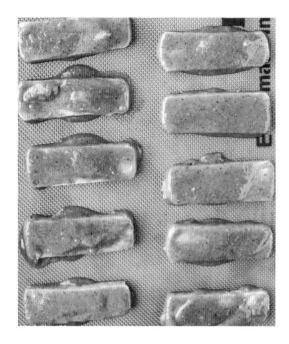

Meanwhile, make the marinade by whisking together the pumpkin, maple syrup, ginger, mustard, nutmeg, cloves, cayenne pepper, and salt and pepper, to taste, in a medium bowl; set aside. (Marinade can be prepared up to 24 hours before using.)

Slice the pressed tofu into 12 to 14 thin slices and place slices in the marinade. Very gently spoon the marinade over the slices and turn them to coat evenly. They are fragile, so do this very tenderly and carefully. Allow slices to marinate for at least 20 minutes, or up to 12 hours. You can let them marinate for the day while you're at work, which makes for an almost work-free dinner that night; cover and refrigerate if you're marinating for many hours.

Prepare a baking sheet by lining it with aluminum foil and spray with cooking spray. I use a nonstick silicone baking mat, although technically you're not supposed to broil with them. Do not bake on an unlined baking tray unless you love cleaning really stubborn blackened and baked-on bits; set aside.

Turn broiler to high and position a rack on the top slot or second slot from the top of the oven.

Place marinated slices on the prepared tray and broil for about 7 minutes, or until edges are just beginning to darken, with 9 minutes likely being the maximum. Watch your tofu the entire time; the tofu can and will burn in a matter of seconds, so it's important to keep a very watchful eye on it.

Tip: To ensure even broiling, I keep the oven door closed for the first 5 minutes of broiling. Then I rotate the tray and stand with the oven door ajar for about 2 more minutes. I rotate the tray a few times over those 2 minutes to find the sweet spot of my broiler's heat and direct it onto the pieces that need it.

Allow tofu to cool on tray for about 5 minutes before serving.

Tofu will keep airtight in the refrigerator for up to 5 days. The tofu can be served either warm or chilled.

Serving suggestion: Dice the tofu and combine with rice or quinoa and other diced vegetables like bell peppers, carrots, snow peas, or corn. Toss with a simple balsamic and oil-based dressing; serve warm or chilled.

Cajun-Spiced Roasted Pumpkin Seeds

You'll never throw away your pumpkin seeds again after trying this easy recipe for roasting them. These crispy, crunchy seeds have a kick, but you can dial down the spices and seasonings if you prefer a milder heat. In case you haven't just carved a pumpkin, the recipe works perfectly well using raw, whole, store-bought seeds. But if I'm working with fresh pumpkin, I like knowing that I used every last bit, even the seeds.

PREP: 5 MINUTES   **COOK:** ABOUT 45 MINUTES

MAKES ABOUT 2 CUPS

2 cups raw, whole pumpkin seeds, cleaned
   and dried (see note)

2 teaspoons melted butter or olive/canola/
   vegetable oil

1 teaspoon Worcestershire sauce

1 teaspoon Sriracha, optional

1 teaspoon maple syrup

2 teaspoons Cajun seasoning

2 teaspoons smoked paprika

½ teaspoon salt

¼ teaspoon cayenne, optional

Note: If seeds are coming straight out of a pumpkin, wash them well and let them air-dry for up to 24 hours on a baking sheet. When roasted, sugar-pumpkin seeds will tend to be crunchier and crispier than carving-pumpkin seeds.

Tip: Boil fresh pumpkin seeds for about 10 minutes in lightly salted water; they'll be easier to clean and crispier when roasted.

Line a baking sheet with a nonstick silicone baking mat or parchment; set aside.

Place seeds in a medium bowl; set aside.

In a small bowl, whisk together the butter, Worcestershire sauce, Sriracha, and maple syrup.

Whisk in the remaining dry seasonings. Pour mixture over seeds and toss to coat.

Spread seeds in a flat, even layer on prepared tray and bake, stirring seeds every 10 to 15 minutes. Continue to bake until outer seed is very golden brown, crispy, and crunchy; inner seed should have only a hint of golden color; if browned it will taste burnt.

Total baking time is usually about 45 minutes. The moisture content of seeds varies dramatically, however, so watch your seeds, not the clock, and stir frequently to prevent them from burning.

Allow seeds to cool on baking tray before transferring to an airtight container. Seeds will keep at room temperature for many weeks.

Drinks and Dips

DIY Pumpkin Pie Spice

Making your own pumpkin pie spice is as easy as combining five spices and stirring them together. The ratio of spices used is a matter of personal preference; feel free to tinker to your liking. The beauty of making your own blend is that you get to customize it according to taste. Not to mention, the last time I checked, a 1.7-ounce jar of a national brand of pumpkin pie spice was more than eight dollars at the grocery store!

Provided you keep these spices on hand anyway, it literally costs pennies to make your own. And now you'll never be out of pumpkin pie spice. So you can bake more pies—or more anything. This makes a great little hostess gift, too.

TIME: 5 MINUTES

MAKES ABOUT 1.5 OUNCES

3 tablespoons cinnamon

2 teaspoons ground allspice

2 teaspoons ground ginger

2 teaspoons ground nutmeg

1½ teaspoons ground cloves

Put the spices in a small bowl and stir to combine.

Transfer mixture to a repurposed spice jar with lid (don't use something that used to store garlic, curry, onion powder, or similar) or use a small glass canning jar or container with a lid.

Tip: To transfer spice mixture into jar, place the mixture on a creased sheet of parchment paper and carefully slide it in, or use a funnel.

Spice mixture will keep airtight at room temperature for many months. Check with each usage to make sure it's fresh and fragrant, especially if you typically bake with pumpkin pie spice on a seasonal basis only.

Pumpkin Syrup

Use a couple of tablespoons of this sweet, pumpkin-spiced syrup when making lattes, specialty coffee drinks, hot cocoa, almond milk, or smoothies. Drizzle it over pancakes, waffles, cinnamon rolls, and cake, or incorporate it into a batch of frosting. Use it anywhere you'd typically use maple syrup or honey, but want the flavors and spices of pumpkin. It's handy to keep a jar in the fridge because it pairs well with so many recipes. Feel free to play with the spice ratios to your taste.

PREP: 5 MINUTES   **COOK:** 10 MINUTES

MAKES ABOUT 1½ CUPS

1 cup granulated sugar

1 cup water

2 tablespoons pumpkin purée

1 teaspoon cinnamon

1 teaspoon pumpkin pie spice

½ teaspoon ground nutmeg

½ teaspoon ground cloves

½ teaspoon ground ginger

Combine sugar and water in a medium saucepan. Cook over medium heat, whisking constantly until sugar is dissolved.

Add pumpkin and spices and whisk to incorporate.

Cook for about 10 minutes, stirring frequently so mixture does not come to a boil. Mixture will thicken and reduce in volume.

Turn off the heat and allow syrup to cool in the pan for about 15 minutes before transferring to a glass jar or heat-safe container with a lid.

Optionally, strain syrup through a coffee filter or cheesecloth before transferring to jar, to remove undissolved spices. This requires patience because the liquid is thick and will take quite a while to strain; I don't bother.

Syrup will keep airtight in the refrigerator for at least 1 month.

Pumpkin-Spice Latte

I have a recipe for pumpkin spice lattes on my website, and every year from August to December it's one of the most popular recipes on my site. With this recipe, there's no need to wait around for seasonally available, high-priced coffeeshop pumpkin spice lattes. You can make them at home for a fraction of the cost.

Although technically lattes are made from steamed milk and espresso shots in roughly a 4:1 ratio, fear not if you don't have an espresso machine or milk steamer. This version uses strong coffee and warmed milk.

The recipe is gluten-free, can easily be kept vegan, and is made with natural ingredients rather than artificially flavored syrups. Because of this, trace amounts of undissolved spices may settle at the bottom of your mug.

TIME: 5 MINUTES

MAKES 1 LARGE LATTE

About ½ cup half-and-half or milk (almond, rice, soy, or cow's milk), warmed

3 to 4 tablespoons pumpkin syrup (page 120)

1+ tablespoon liquid sweetener (agave, maple syrup, honey), optional

½ teaspoon vanilla extract

1 cup+ freshly brewed strong coffee

Whipped topping for garnishing, optional

Pinch pumpkin pie spice for garnishing, optional

Pour milk into a large microwave-safe glass measuring cup and heat until warmed, but not boiling, about 45 seconds.

Whisk in the pumpkin syrup, sweetener, if using, to taste, and vanilla.

Pour coffee into a mug. Top with the milky mixture. Stir to combine.

If desired, garnish with whipped topping and pumpkin pie spice. Serve immediately.

Gingerbread Pumpkin-Pie and Irish Cream Martini

I love Irish cream liquor (think Baileys) so much that I created a homemade DIY version, which I posted on my website a few years ago. This martini combines my love of Irish cream and pumpkin, and pairs them with gingerbread cookies. It's like drinking an Irish cream–infused pumpkin pie, complete with gingerbread crust. They go down very easily.

TIME: 5 MINUTES

MAKES 1 MARTINI, EASILY DOUBLED

About 3 small gingerbread cookies, speculoos, or cinnamon graham crackers, crushed, for rimming glasses and optional garnish

About ½ teaspoon corn syrup or honey, for rimming glasses

2 parts (about 1½ ounces) pumpkin-flavored vodka (such as Pinnacle Pumpkin Pie Vodka), chilled

2 parts (about 1½ ounce) Irish cream liquor (Baileys is delicious here)

Splash half-and-half, cream, or pumpkin-flavored coffee creamer

Pinch pumpkin pie spice, plus more for garnishing if desired

Whipped cream, optional, for garnishing

Place cookies in a small ziploc sandwich bag, seal it, and using a spoon or rolling pin, gently crush cookies into crumbs (some larger bits are okay for optional garnishing). Transfer crumbs to a plate.

Using your finger, line inner and outer edge of martini glass with corn syrup or honey so cookie crumbs adhere to rim. Dip glass in crumbs to coat evenly.

Add vodka, Irish cream, half-and-half, and pumpkin pie spice to the glass, and stir gently to combine. Serve immediately. Optionally, garnish with whipped cream, a sprinkle of cinnamon, nutmeg, or pumpkin pie spice, and/or leftover cookie crumbs.

Creamy Pumpkin-Spice Almond Milk

Making your own almond milk is incredibly easy, and after you've tasted homemade, store-bought just can't compare. It's as easy as soaking almonds, blending with water, and adding sweetener and spices. The milk is creamy and rich, and you'd never guess it's plant-based and vegan, perfect for those with dairy intolerance. The milk is wonderful in smoothies and milk shakes, and I like to add a splash to tea or coffee. Depending on preferences, tinker with the sweetener and spice ratios, or try other fall-flavored spices like cloves, ginger, or nutmeg. Cashews can also be substituted for the almonds, creating some of the creamiest and richest nut milk.

PREP: 10 MINUTES   **TOTAL:** 4+ HOURS, FOR SOAKING

MAKES ABOUT 4 CUPS (32 OUNCES)

1 cup raw almonds (unroasted, unsalted)

3 cups water for soaking, plus 3 to 4 cups for blending

2 to 4 tablespoons+ agave, honey, brown rice syrup, maple syrup, pinch stevia, or preferred sweetener

1 teaspoon pumpkin pie spice

½ teaspoon cinnamon

1 teaspoon vanilla extract, optional

2 to 4+ tablespoons pumpkin purée, optional (see note)

Note: Pumpkin purée may be added along with the sweetener and spices to boost flavor; starting with 2 to 4 tablespoons, adjust to taste as desired. Since it does not dissolve, pumpkin purée thickens the almond milk considerably and adds bulk. This is fine if you plan to use the almond milk for pumpkin milk-shakes or smoothies, such as Pumpkin-Pie-In-A-Cup (page 128). However, for other applications, you may not want the milk to be as thick.

In the canister of a blender, cover almonds with about 3 cups water, put the lid on, and allow almonds to soak at room temperature for at least 4 hours; overnight (8 to 24 hours) is optimal.

Drain nuts and rinse momentarily under running water. Some of the skins may have loosened; this is a good sign.

Return almonds to blender canister, add 3 to 4 cups water (I prefer 3½ to 4 cups total), and blend for at least 3 minutes on high speed, until mixture is as smooth and fine as your blender can get it.

Place a nut-milk bag filter or cheesecloth over a large bowl or pitcher. Slowly pour the almond milk into the bag or over the cheesecloth. Squeeze the bag to release the milk. It takes a few minutes for all the milk to release and drain. Discard the pulp (alternatively, reserve pulp for use in other recipes; search for "almond pulp" online for ideas).

Note: Nut-milk bags are available online or in many natural food grocery stores. They're inexpensive and reusable. Although straining the milk through a nut-milk bag or cheesecloth produces a smoother-textured milk with less pulp, if you don't have one or don't object to pulp, it's fine to skip this step, noting that milk will be thicker.

Rinse blender canister and pour strained almond milk into it. Add sweetener, pumpkin pie spice, cinnamon, and vanilla and pumpkin purée, if using, and blend. Taste the milk and play with the sweetener and spice ratios, to taste.

Transfer almond milk to glass jar or other vessel with a lid that can be sealed. Store milk airtight in the refrigerator for 4 to 5 days. Shake very well prior to using.

Pumpkin-Pie-in-a-Cup Smoothie

If you've ever wanted to drink a slice of pumpkin pie, this is your chance. The bonus is that this treat is healthier than pie, just in case you're in holiday-dessert overload. The smoothie is creamy, rich, vegan, gluten-free, and takes just a minute to blend together. It's a perfect quickie breakfast, post-workout treat, or afternoon pick-me-up. The pumpkin and yogurt are filling, and this thick smoothie is satisfying and healthy.

TIME: 3 MINUTES

MAKES ABOUT 12 OUNCES

Tip: Double the batch and freeze the leftovers. Although mixture becomes a bit crystallized, after 5 minutes at room temperature, it's a lower-calorie frozen treat option than Bourbon Pumpkin Ice Cream (page 84).

About ¾ cup milk (use almond milk to keep the recipe vegan; try Creamy Pumpkin-Spice Almond Milk, page 126)

½ heaping cup pumpkin purée, chilled

½ cup thick Greek yogurt, plain, vanilla, or pumpkin-flavored

⅓ cup Pumpkin Syrup (page 120)

2 tablespoons maple syrup, optional

¾ teaspoon pumpkin pie spice, plus a pinch for garnishing

Whipped cream (use coconut whipped cream to keep it vegan), optional, for garnishing

Combine milk, pumpkin, yogurt, pumpkin syrup, maple syrup, if using, and pumpkin pie spice in a blender and blend until smooth and creamy. Add more or less milk depending on how thick or thin you prefer your smoothies.

If desired, top with whipped cream and a pinch of pumpkin pie spice. Serve immediately.

Variations
- Add a small banana or previously frozen banana chunks for a creamier, thicker smoothie. The banana flavor is only slightly noticeable, not as much as you might think. I love using bananas in smoothies and usually toss one in.
- Add 2 to 4 tablespoons instant pudding mix—try vanilla, French vanilla, cheesecake, or similar flavors. The pudding will thicken the smoothie, but also adds sweetness, so omit the maple syrup or smoothie will be too sweet.

Chocolaty Pumpkin Hot Chocolate

You know those hot chocolate packets that contain chocolate powder, sugar, chemicals, preservatives, and mini marshmallows that look like freeze-dried outer space food? You don't need to buy those anymore. Make this instead, in almost the same amount of time and with almost no effort.

It's very chocolaty thanks to both the cocoa powder and dark chocolate, but I won't apologize for extra-chocolaty hot chocolate that's rich and creamy. You probably won't mind. It hits the spot after a chilly day outside; sip it by the fireplace or curled up on the couch, remote in one hand and mug in the other. I like to spike mine with a splash of Irish cream liquor to help boost the warm-and-toasty effect.

TIME: 5 MINUTES

MAKES ABOUT 12 OUNCES (SERVES 1 GENEROUSLY, OR 2 MORE MODESTLY)

⅓ cup water

2 tablespoons Pumpkin Syrup (page 120)

2 tablespoons unsweetened natural cocoa powder (Dutch-processed may be substituted)

2 tablespoons granulated sugar

1 ounce semi-sweet or dark chocolate, chopped (I prefer 54–72 percent cacao)

¾ cup milk or half-and-half (to keep recipe vegan, use almond, soy, or coconut milk)

Marshmallows or whipped cream, optional, for garnishing

Chocolate shavings, optional, for garnishing

Pinch pumpkin pie spice, optional, for garnishing

Combine water, pumpkin syrup, cocoa powder, sugar, and chocolate in a small saucepan and heat over medium heat to melt and dissolve ingredients, whisking constantly.

As soon as mixture has melted and is smooth and just begins to boil, slowly pour in the milk, whisking constantly.

Heat for another 30 to 60 seconds, or long enough to be nicely warmed through, without boiling; whisk nearly constantly.

Pour into a mug, garnish as desired, and serve immediately.

Coconut Cream Pumpkin-Pie Shooters

These little shooters are creamy, smooth, easy to knock back, and combine two of my favorite pies in one. They're fun to set out at holiday parties or as a nice end to a festive meal in lieu of dessert. Think of them as pie in a shotglass. Or serve them with dessert. You can never have too many desserts.

TIME: 5 MINUTES

MAKES 2 OR 3 SHOOTERS

Ice cubes

2 ounces pumpkin pie vodka (such as Pinnacle Pumpkin Pie Vodka)

2 ounces whipped cream vodka (such as Pinnacle or Smirnoff) or vanilla vodka (regular vodka may be substituted)

2 ounces cream of coconut (such as Coco Lopez)

½ teaspoon pumpkin pie spice

Whipped cream, optional for garnishing

Fill a cocktail shaker halfway with ice cubes. Add the vodkas, cream of coconut, and pumpkin pie spice and shake well.

Pour mixture into shotglasses, and optionally garnish with whipped cream. Serve immediately.

Cinnamon-and-Spice Pumpkin Cream Cheese

Long after the seasonally available pumpkin cream cheese spreads are gone from store shelves for the year, you can make your own in minutes, any time of the year. What better way to enjoy toast or bagels than with a big schmear of pumpkin-flavored cream cheese?

TIME: 5 MINUTES

MAKES ABOUT 4 OUNCES; RECIPE IS EASILY DOUBLED

4 ounces cream cheese, softened
    (light or fat-free is okay)
2 tablespoons pumpkin purée
1 teaspoon cinnamon
1 teaspoon pumpkin pie spice
1 teaspoon granulated sugar, optional

In a small bowl, combine cream cheese, pumpkin, cinnamon, pumpkin pie spice, and sugar, if using, and whisk together by hand or beat with an electric mixer until smooth.

Serve with toast, bagels, muffins, crackers, or anything you enjoy smearing with cream cheese.

Cream cheese will keep airtight in the refrigerator for up to 10 days.

Fluffy Creamy Pumpkin-Pie Dip

I love dips of all kinds, and the fluffier and creamier the better. The closer I can get to eating frosting or pie filling by smearing it on crackers and calling it a dip, the happier I am. I don't even need crackers or fresh fruit slices for this fast and easy dip that comes together in minutes. I'm quite content just digging in with a spoon.

TIME: 5 MINUTES

MAKES ABOUT 2 CUPS; RECIPE IS EASILY DOUBLED (SEE NOTE)

1 cup pumpkin purée

4 ounces (half a tub) whipped topping, thawed (Cool Whip or similar; light or fat-free is okay)

2 ounces (about ¼ cup) cream cheese, softened (light or fat-free is okay)

½ cup confectioners' sugar

1 teaspoon pumpkin pie spice

Note: To double, use a whole tub of whipped topping, a full 15-ounce can of pumpkin purée, and double the other ingredients.

In a large bowl, combine pumpkin, whipped topping, cream cheese, confectioners' sugar, and pumpkin pie spice and beat with an electric mixer until smooth, or whisk by hand.

Serve immediately with graham crackers, cookies, bagels, apple or pear slices, pretzels, or your favorite snack foods. Dip will keep airtight in the refrigerator for up to 1 week.

Acknowledgments

This book would not have been possible without my having readers for it. To those who have bought a book, thank you for your support. You are the most important person! This includes Averie Cooks blog readers and those who are just now picking up the book because you love pumpkin as much as I do.

Thank you to my precious six-year-old, Skylar, for being the best little girl I could ever dream of. For understanding what it meant when I said I had to work on the book and couldn't come to the park with you that day, or many, many days. You are the most patient child I could ever ask for, and I love you so much. And you also ate more pumpkin over the past year than any kid I know. Thank you.

Thank you to Scott, for seeing me through another book and for playing the role of Daddy Dearest for months on end while I cooked, photographed, and wrote my heart out. They say it takes a village to raise a child. It definitely takes a father like you while the mother is knee-deep in pumpkin purée. Thank you for eating every single thing in this book, many times over. I promise I wasn't trying to turn you orange.

Thank you to my parents, Paul and Marsha, and my sister, Claire, for raising me in a house where cooking happened daily, where the food that was on the dinner table mattered and was important, and where being together as a family and sharing was even more important. It's slightly ironic that I've become a food blogger, food writer, and cookbook author, but it really isn't surprising after reflecting upon the fundamentals and old-fashioned values that you instilled. Thank you.

Thank you to Holly for finding me. You got this whole big ball of pumpkin rolling. Although we had more twists and turns than one of those giant corn mazes, thank you for always believing in me, the book, and seeing it through.

Thank you to the team at W. W. Norton, especially my editors, Ann and Lisa. After the first time Ann and I talked on the phone, I just knew it was meant to be. Thank you for seeing the promise in pumpkin and for knowing that pumpkin could be more than just pie filling and for allowing this book to become a reality. Thank you for giving me the space and creative license to write it the way I wanted to, and for having faith in me as a cook, recipe developer, writer, and photographer. Your support and confidence in me has been such a wonderful gift.

MEASUREMENT CONVERSION TABLES

The following tables provide equivalents for U.S. and metric (U.K.) units of measure. Values have been rounded up or down to the nearest whole number.

VOLUME

U.S.	METRIC
1 teaspoon	5 milliliters
1 tablespoon	15 milliliters
¼ cup	59 milliliters
⅓ cup	79 milliliters
½ cup	118 milliliters
¾ cup	177 milliliters
1 cup	237 milliliters
4 cups (1 quart)	.95 liter
1.06 quarts	1 liter
4 quarts (1 gallon)	3.8 liters

WEIGHT

OUNCES	GRAMS
½	14
1	28
8	227
12	340
16 (1 pound)	454

COMMON BAKING INGREDIENTS

INGREDIENT	OUNCES	GRAMS
1 cup all-purpose flour	5	142
1 cup cake flour	4	113
1 cup whole wheat flour	5½	156
1 cup granulated (white) sugar	7	198
1 cup packed brown sugar (light or dark)	7	198
1 cup confectioners' sugar	4	113
1 cup cocoa powder	3	85
8 tablespoons butter (1 stick, or ½ cup)	4	113

COOKING TEMPERATURE/DEGREES

To convert Fahrenheit to Celsius, subtract 32 from the Fahrenheit temperature, then divide the result by 1.8 to find the Celsius equivalent.

Index